The Spanish-American War

The Spanish-American War

KENNETH E. HENDRICKSON JR.

Greenwood Guides to Historic Events 1500–1900
Linda S. Frey and Marsha L. Frey, Series Editors

GREENWOOD PRESS
Westport, Connecticut • London

Library of Congress Cataloging-in-Publication Data

Hendrickson, Kenneth E.
    The Spanish-American War / Kenneth E. Hendrickson, Jr.
        p. cm.—(Greenwood guides to historic events, 1500–1900,
    ISSN 1538-442X)
    Includes bibliographical references and index.
    ISBN 0–313–31662–7 (alk. paper)
    1. Spanish-American War, 1898. I. Title. II. Series.
    E715.H48 2003
    973.8'9—dc21   2003040843

British Library Cataloguing in Publication Data is available.

Library of Congress Catalog Card Number: 2003040843

ISBN: 0–313–31662–7
ISSN: 1538–442X

First published in 2003

Greenwood Press, 88 Post Road West, Westport, CT 06881
An imprint of Greenwood Publishing Group, Inc.
www.greenwood.com

Printed in the United States of America

The paper used in this book complies with the
Permanent Paper Standard issued by the National
Information Standards Organization (Z39.48–1984).

10 9 8 7 6 5 4 3 2 1

The author and publisher gratefully acknowledge the permission to reprint the
following. Excerpts from *The Spanish War: An American Epic,* 1898 by G. L. A. O'Toole.
Copyright © 1984 by G. O'Toole. Used by permission of W. W. Norton & Company,
Inc.

Every reasonable effort has been made to trace the owners of world copyright material
for the above mentioned book, but this has proven impossible. The author and
publisher will be glad to receive information leading to more complete
acknowledgments in subsequent printings of the book and in the meantime extend
their apologies for this omission.

This book is dedicated to the memory of my father,
who was my inspiration,
Kenneth E. Hendrickson Sr.
January 28, 1909–April 24, 2002

CONTENTS

Photo essay follows Chapter 7.

MAPS

SERIES FOREWORD

American statesman Adlai Stevenson stated, "We can chart our future clearly and wisely only when we know the path which has led to the present." This series, *Greenwood Guides to Historic Events, 1500–1900*, is designed to illuminate that path by focusing on events from 1500 to 1900 that have shaped the world. The years 1500 to 1900 include what historians call the Early Modern Period (1500 to 1789, the onset of the French Revolution) and part of the modern period (1789 to 1900).

In 1500, an acceleration of key trends marked the beginnings of an interdependent world and the posing of seminal questions that changed the nature and terms of intellectual debate. The series closes with 1900, the inauguration of the twentieth century. This period witnessed profound economic, social, political, cultural, religious, and military changes. An industrial and technological revolution transformed the modes of production, marked the transition from a rural to an urban economy, and ultimately raised the standard of living. Social classes and distinctions shifted. The emergence of the territorial and later the national state altered man's relations with and view of political authority. The shattering of the religious unity of the Roman Catholic world in Europe marked the rise of a new pluralism. Military revolutions changed the nature of warfare. The books in this series emphasize the complexity and diversity of the human tapestry and include political, economic, social, intellectual, military, and cultural topics. Some of the authors focus on events in U.S. history such as the Salem witchcraft trials, the American Revolution, the abolitionist movement, and the Civil War. Others analyze European topics, such as the Reformation and Counter-Reformation and the French Revolution. Still others bridge cultures and continents by examining the voyages of discovery, the Atlantic slave trade, and the Age of Imperialism. Some focus on intellectual questions that have shaped the modern world, such as Darwin's *Origin of Species,* or on turning points such as the Age of Romanticism. Others examine defining economic, religious, or legal events or issues such as the building of the railroads, the Second Great Awakening, and abolitionism. Heroes (e.g., Lewis and Clark), scientists (e.g., Darwin), military leaders (e.g., Napoleon), and poets (e.g., Byron) stride across its pages. Many of these events were seminal in that they marked profound changes or turning points. The Scientific Revolution, for example, changed the way individuals viewed themselves and their world.

The authors, acknowledged experts in their fields, synthesize key events; set developments within the larger historical context; and, most important, present a well-balanced, well-written account that integrates the most recent scholarship in the field.

The topics were chosen by an advisory board composed of historians, high school history teachers, and school librarians to support the curriculum and meet student research needs. The volumes are designed to serve as resources for student research and to provide clearly written interpretations of topics central to the secondary school and lower-level undergraduate history curriculum. Each author outlines a basic chronology to guide the reader through often confusing events and a historical overview to set those events within a narrative framework. Three to five topical chapters underscore critical aspects of the event. In the final chapter the author examines the impact and consequences of the event. Biographical sketches furnish background on the lives and contributions of the players who strut across this stage. Ten to fifteen primary documents ranging from letters to diary entries, song lyrics, proclamations, and posters cast light on the event, provide material for student essays, and stimulate a critical engagement with the sources. Introductions identify the authors of the documents and the main issues. In some cases a glossary of selected terms is provided as a guide to the reader. Each work contains an annotated bibliography of recommended books, articles, CD-ROMs, Internet sites, videos, and films that set the materials within the historical debate.

These works will lead to a more sophisticated understanding of the events and debates that have shaped the modern world and will stimulate a more active engagement with the issues that still affect us. It has been a particularly enriching experience to work closely with such dedicated professionals. We have come to know and value even more highly the authors in this series and our editors at Greenwood, particularly Barbara Rader and Kevin Ohe. In many cases they have become more than colleagues; they have become friends. To them and to future historians we dedicate this series.

Linda S. Frey
University of Montana

Marsha L. Frey
Kansas State University

PREFACE

The war between the United States and Spain in 1898 receives relatively little attention in most American history texts, yet it was an event of great importance. This country emerged as the world's greatest power in the twentieth century—with all the responsibilities and problems emanating from that status—and the war with Spain was in many ways like a stepping-stone from one era of American history to the next. It confirmed the need for a large and powerful navy; it satisfied—in par at least—the demands of expansionists who believed that economic growth required overseas sources and markets; it confirmed the importance of industrialization; and it brought Americans face-to-face, more forcefully than ever before, with the fact that aggressive nationalism could be both crowned with splendor and fraught with danger.

This volume is designed to introduce both high school and college students to the importance of "the splendid little war" by examining its causes, major events, and long-term implications. It also attempts to present the war from both the American and Spanish points of view to provide a perspective not usually found. The book begins with a chronology of events, followed by an overview of the entire war and several chapters devoted to the major campaigns. Chapter 3 describes the military action in Cuba and Puerto Rico, while chapter 4 deals with the important naval engagements in Manila Bay and in the waters near Santiago de Cuba. Chapter 5 focuses on the campaign in the Philippines, chapter 6 deals with the peace process, and chapter 7 summarizes the long-term significance and consequences of the war in world affairs.

Also included are several biographical sketches of major participants in the military and diplomatic events connected with the war, and
a set of documents. These include official papers, autobiographical
accounts, descriptions of events by participants, newspaper opinions,
and even a satirical approach that was very popular among contemporaries. Finally, an annotated bibliography directs students to further,
more in-depth reading in both secondary and primary sources.

I could not have completed this project without a great deal of
help. Heartfelt thanks are due to my secretary, Kay Hardin; my research
assistant, David H. Gaines; the staff of Moffett Library at Midwestern
State University; and the staff of the Photographic and Print Division at
the Library of Congress. I also want to thank Marsha and Linda Frey,
editors of the series, and Kevin Ohe of Greenwood Press for their
encouragement and support.

CHRONOLOGY
OF EVENTS

1895

February 24   Second Cuban Insurrection began.

April   General Máximo Gómez, General Antonio Maceo, José Martí, and other leaders arrived in Cuba. Actual fighting began.

October 1895– Antonio Maceo and Máximo Gómez took their forces
January 1896 on *La Invasion,* fighting almost every day, from Mangos de Baragua Oriente Province in eastern Cuba to Mantua in Pinar del Rio Province in extreme western Cuba.

1896

January   Antonio Maceo and Máximo Gómez ended *La Invasion.*

February 16   General Weyler issued first of *reconcentrado* orders.

March 24   Calixto García, escaped from Spain, arrived in Cuba with well-armed expedition.

August 26   Philippine Revolution began.

December 7   Antonio Maceo killed in encounter at Punta Brava, Havana Province.

1897

March 4   William McKinley inaugurated as president of the United States.

June 19   Stewart Woodford appointed U.S. minister to Spain.

August 8   Spanish prime minister Canovas assassinated.

August 30	The Spanish forts at Tunas, in northwestern Oriente Province, fell to Calixto García.
October 4	Prime Minister Sagasta took office in Spain.
October 31	Prime Minister Sagasta recalled General Weyler from Cuba.
November 28	The Spanish forts at Guisa, in the northern foothills of Sierra Maestra Oriente Province, fell to Calixto García.

1898

January 1	Spain instituted limited political autonomy in Cuba.
January 12	Spanish in Cuba "rioted," or demonstrated against autonomy. Consul-General Fitzhugh Lee took this as a threat against Americans.
January 17	Consul-General Lee asked for ship to be sent to Havana.
January 21	Esperanza, the Cuban rebel stronghold, was invaded.
January 24	President McKinley sent battleship *Maine* to Havana.
January 25	Battleship *Maine* arrived in Havana.
February 1	Spanish forces were defeated at Rejondon de Baguanos. This, and other previous operations by Garcia, caused the Spanish to abandon the strategically important interior of Oriente Province and effectively isolated Santiago de Cuba by land from other coastal Spanish garrisons.
February 9	The Dupuy de Lôme letter, critical of McKinley, was printed, causing the Spanish diplomat to be recalled.
February 15	Battleship *Maine* exploded; 266 crewmen killed.
February 16	Dupuy de Lôme left the United States for Spain.
February 17	Naval Board of Inquiry into the loss of the battleship *Maine* (the Sampson Board) established.
February 18	Spanish cruiser *Vizcaya* arrived in New York in reciprocal visit for the USS *Maine,* unaware that the *Maine* had been lost.
February 21	The Naval Court of Inquiry into the loss of the *Maine* began.
February 25	*Vizcaya* left New York for Havana.

March 6	Spain requested, unofficially, that Consul-General Lee be recalled.
March 8	Congress authorized $50 million for a war fund.
March 12	Battleship *Oregon,* under Captain Charles Clark, left San Francisco for Florida, by way of Tierra del Fuego, on its famous dash.
March 14	Admiral Cervera's squadron steamed for the Cape Verde Islands.
March 21	Board of Inquiry Report was completed; concluded that battleship *Maine* lost to a mine.
March 25	McKinley received Board of Inquiry Report.
March 26	McKinley sent note to Spain demanding an end to the war in Cuba, as well as a note indicating the findings of the Naval Board of Inquiry.
March 28	Naval Court of Inquiry report was presented to Congress. On the same day, the report of the Spanish Board of Inquiry into the loss of the *Maine* was received in Washington. Report stated that the loss was the result of an internal accident.
March 30	U.S. minister to Spain Woodford requested that war in Cuba end and that Cuba be given independence.
March 31	Spain rejected demands for Cuban independence.
April 1	U.S. House of Representatives authorized $226 million for naval vessels.
April 6	Pope asked McKinley not to declare war pending the Pope's negotiations with Spain.
April 7	Ambassadors of England, Germany, France, Italy, Austria, and Russia appealed to McKinley for peace.
April 9	Spain ordered General Blanco to declare armistice in Cuba. Consul-General Lee and other U.S. citizens left Cuba.
April 11	McKinley asked Congress for war.
April 16	Army began mobilization. Teller Amendment passed in United States Congress, stating that the United States would not annex Cuba.
April 19	U.S. Congress declared Cuba independent.

April 22	U.S. navy commenced blockade of Cuba.
April 23	McKinley issued a call for 125,000 volunteers. Spain declared war.
April 25	United States declared war but made the declaration retroactive to April 22.
April 27	Commodore Dewey's squadron left Mirs Bay, China, for the Philippines.
April 29	Calixto García took Bayamo, abandoned by the Spanish, as headquarters.
April 30	Admiral Cervera's Spanish squadron left the Cape Verde Islands for the Caribbean.
May 1	U.S. navy's Asiatic Squadron under Commodore Dewey defeated the Spanish Pacific Squadron at the Battle of Manila Bay.
May 11	Dewey promoted to rear admiral.
May 12	Admiral Sampson bombarded San Juan, Puerto Rico, without warning.
May 13	Commodore Schley's Flying Squadron left Hampton Roads for the vicinity of Cuba.
May 15	Theodore Roosevelt began training with Rough Riders.
May 17	Cervera's squadron arrived in Santiago, Cuba.
May 22	Battleship *Oregon* arrived off Florida after the 14,700-nautical-mile dash from the U.S. west coast.
May 29	U.S. navy blockaded Spanish fleet in Santiago harbor.
May 31	Schley and the blockading squadron skirmished with *Cristóbal Colón* and shelled the forts at Santiago.
June 3	Lieutenant Richmond P. Hobson sank the *Merrimac* at the entrance to Santiago harbor.
June 10	U.S. marines landed at Guantanamo Bay in Cuba.
June 12–14	Major-General Shafter's Fifth Corps embarked at Tampa.
June 15	Spanish squadron left Spain for the Philippines.
June 21	Guam "captured" by U.S. forces.
June 20	Calixto García met with U.S. general William Shafter in Asseradero Sierra Maestra to coordinate U.S. landings.

June 22	Fifth Corps of 16,000 men landed at Daiquiri in Cuba throughout the day.
June 22–23	Cuban scouts take about 20 wounded and report to General Lawton that the first strong Spanish positions are at La Guasimas. Lawton ordered U.S. and Cuban forces at his command to hold positions, before formal attack.
June 24	Battle of Las Guasimas.
July 1	Battles of El Caney and San Juan Hill.
July 3	Spanish fleet attempted to escape from Santiago; all ships destroyed at the naval Battle of Santiago.
July 6	Hobson and his crew were exchanged for Spanish prisoners.
July 8	Spanish squadron heading for the Philippines was forced to turn around to protect the Spanish coastline.
July 10	Santiago bombarded by the U.S. navy.
July 17	Spanish Santiago garrison surrendered.
July 25	U.S. army invaded Puerto Rico.
July 26	Spanish asked for terms of peace through the French ambassador.
July 31	Night attack by the Spanish on the American lines at Manila.
August 9	Battle of Caomo, Puerto Rico, resulted in U.S. victory; Spain accepted McKinley's terms of peace.
August 11	American troops entered Mayaguez, Puerto Rico's third-largest city.
August 12	Peace protocol was signed (truce).
August 13	U.S. forces took Manila with a minor fight.
August 20	Large naval review in New York Harbor.
August 23	General Merritt was appointed governor of Manila. Command of Eighth Corps in Philippines given to General Otis.
August 25	General Shafter left Cuba.
September 10	Spanish Cortes approved peace protocol.
September 12	Admiral Cervera left United States to return to Spain.

September 13 Rough Riders mustered out of service; Spanish senate approved peace protocol.

September 14 U.S. troops began leaving Puerto Rico; queen regent of Spain signed peace protocol.

September 20 First U.S. flag was raised in Havana, Cuba.

September 24 Leonard Wood was made military governor of Cuba.

September 29 Spanish and American peace commissioners met for the first time.

October 12 *Oregon* and *Iowa* left New York for Manila.

October 18 United States took formal possession of Puerto Rico.

November 28 Spain agreed to cede Philippines Islands.

November 30 General Blanco left Cuba for Spain.

December 10 Treaty of Paris ended war.

December 23 Aguinaldo's cabinet resigned in the Philippines.

1899
February 4 Philippine Insurrection began.

1901
March 4 McKinley's second inauguration, with Roosevelt as vice president.

March 23 Philippine revolutionary leader General Aguinaldo was captured.

September 14 McKinley died after being shot on September 6; Theodore Roosevelt became president.

1902
July 4 Roosevelt declared the Philippines pacified.

CHAPTER 1

BACKGROUND AND OVERVIEW OF THE SPANISH-AMERICAN WAR

The Spanish-American War in 1898 resulted from a U.S. policy that emerged quickly in the mid-1890s and held that Spain could no longer be permitted to control the island of Cuba and that the United States was prepared to use force to bring about the desired change. This attitude represented a significant departure from American policies that were in place earlier in the nineteenth century; hence a discussion of these earlier policies is necessary to place the war in the proper historical perspective.

From the 1820s until 1849 the dominant feature of U.S. policy in the Caribbean was to guarantee Spanish sovereignty over Cuba. The United States, fearing British and French ambitions in the Caribbean, opposed the transfer of Cuba or any other nearby island or region to any power stronger than Spain. The United States especially wanted Cuba and Puerto Rico to remain under Spain's feeble control until such time, it was hoped, they would simply drift into American hands.

After the annexation of Texas in 1845 and the conquests of the Mexican War in 1848, the direction of American policy changed. Now the goal was acquisition of the island, a reflection of the widely held belief in that era known as Manifest Destiny. The idea behind Manifest Destiny was that it was God's will that the Americans should control most—if not all—of the North American continent and the Caribbean. The concept also included a belief in the superiority of American institutions, utter contempt for the decadent monarchies of Europe, and a strong sense of righteousness about any aggressive action the nation might undertake to achieve its goals. The result was that by the middle of the nineteenth century, American policy became much more aggressive and intolerant and now threatened rather than defended Spanish sovereignty in Cuba.

Inevitably, the Cuban question became entangled with the greater issue of the expansion of slavery during the 1850s. Responding to the demands of proslavery expansionist Democrats, President James K. Polk offered to pay as much as $100 million to buy Cuba from Spain in June 1848, but the offer was rebuffed. Spanish public opinion, as reflected in the newspapers of the day, overwhelmingly opposed the idea.

In the early 1850s, during the administrations of Zachary Taylor and Millard Fillmore, the proslavery expansionists could not obtain official support for the annexation of Cuba because of tension gener-ated by the debate over slavery. Some expansionists, therefore, turned to filibustering. A filibustering expedition was a privately organized and financed, unofficial and unsanctioned paramilitary effort to detach Cuba from Spain and ultimately bring it into the union. The leading fil-ibusterer of this period was Narciso Lopez, a Cuban exile who lived in the United States. His plan was to raise an army of Americans and other Cuban exiles who would invade Cuba and rouse the people to revolt against Spain. Most of his support in the United States came from Southerners who very much wanted to bring Cuba into the union as a slave state.

On three occasions, in 1849, 1850, and 1851, Lopez attempted to launch his invasion. In 1849, American authorities stopped him before he could leave New York. The following year, departing from New Orleans, he landed in Cuba, but the people did not rise up to join him as he had expected and he was forced to flee. His third effort in 1851 was a complete disaster. He landed in northern Cuba near Havana but fell into a Spanish trap. Nearly all his men were killed in the battle while Lopez himself, and others who were captured, were executed.

The failure of the Lopez expedition, and especially the execution of the prisoners, enraged Southerners. In New Orleans and Mobile, Alabama, anti-Spain riots took place and Spanish property was dam-aged. The Spanish government demanded satisfaction, and in 1852 the United States apologized and paid for some of the damages. Meanwhile, Spain sought help from European powers to defend against further incursions. Neither Britain nor France wanted to intervene directly, but in 1852 they proposed that the United States join with them in a three-power treaty declaring that none of them would try to acquire Cuba. Before the treaty could be approved, the presidential elections brought victory to Democrat Franklin Pierce. Although he was a Northerner, Pierce sympathized with the South and with the expansionists. Hence the treaty was rejected.

President Pierce openly favored the acquisition of Cuba and appointed avowed expansionists to important cabinet and diplomatic posts. Among these were William L. Marcy, secretary of state, and Pierre Soulé, minister to Spain. Soulé had been a great fan of Lopez, and he believed that his primary goal as minister to Spain should be the acquisition of Cuba. New filibusters also appeared early in the Pierce administration. The most important of these was John A. Quitman, an extreme proslavery Southerner from Mississippi. He dreamed of creating a great southern empire of slavery that would include not only Cuba but also Mexico. Supposedly, Quitman had raised a war chest of more than a million dollars, had an army of 50,000 men, and was well armed. These figures may be exaggerated, but there is no doubt that Quitman intended to invade Cuba. President Pierce wanted to support him, but the politics of the slavery controversy made it difficult to do so.

Two developments forced Quitman to abandon his scheme. The first was an incident known as the *Black Warrior* affair, and the second was the passage by Congress of the Kansas-Nebraska Act. The *Black Warrior* was an American steamship whose cargo was seized in Cuba for violation of port regulations. At first this appeared to be just the incident needed as an excuse for war and the seizure of Cuba by force. Secretary Marcy instructed Soulé to demand an apology and an indemnity of $300,000, but Soulé went beyond his instructions. He issued the demand for an indemnity as a forty-eight-hour ultimatum. The Spanish foreign minister, suspecting that Soulé had exceeded his authority, ignored the ultimatum, and Spain settled directly with the owners of the ship. Pierce went along with the settlement because of the uproar caused by the passage of the Kansas-Nebraska Act.

The Kansas-Nebraska Act was one of the most inflammatory bills Congress ever passed. Originally, the idea was simply to organize a territorial government in the northern part of the Louisiana Purchase, then known as Nebraska, to make it more attractive to build a transcontinental railroad through the region. To secure Southern support, Senator Stephen A. Douglas (D-Illinois) and other promoters of the bill agreed to divide the region into two parts, allow the settlers in the Southern area (Kansas) to vote on the question of allowing slavery, and to repeal the provision of the Missouri Compromise (1821) that prohibited slavery north of latitude 36°30'. Pierce favored the bill, but it inspired such intense opposition in the North that he did not dare launch a war to grab Cuba at the same time. On June 1, 1854, the day after he signed the Kansas-Nebraska Act, Pierce issued a presidential proclamation declaring that the U.S. government would prosecute anyone who violated the neutrality laws. This act crushed Quitman's plans once and for all.

The end of filibustering, however, did not end U.S. interest in Cuba. Now Pierce shifted back to the idea of purchasing the island. In April 1854, the president authorized Pierre Soulé to offer Spain $130 million for Cuba. Because this effort failed, in August Secretary Marcy instructed Soulé to confer with James Buchanan, U.S. minister to Great Britain, and John Y. Mason, U.S. minister to France, to decide what might be done next. Soulé, Buchanan, and Mason concocted a proposal that came to be known as the Ostend Manifesto because some of their meetings took place in Ostend, Belgium. In this document they repeated all the arguments favoring U.S. acquisition of Cuba. If Spain declined to sell the island, they argued, the United States would be justified in seizing it by force. Although the manifesto was supposed to be secret, news of it leaked out and generated a very unfavorable reaction in both Europe and the United States. About the same time, the Democrats suffered defeats in the congressional election, and because these reversals appeared to be caused in part by the administration's aggressive Cuban policy, Pierce backed down. Soulé was instructed to cease his efforts immediately, and he resigned.

These difficulties did not end the Democrats' interest in Cuba. In 1856 James Buchanan, the Democratic candidate for president, won on a platform that included a demand for the annexation of Cuba. On three occasions during his one term Buchanan called upon Congress to approve annexation, but he failed each time because the desire to acquire Cuba still appeared to advance the interests of slavery. The outbreak of the Civil War in 1861 brought an end to expansionist efforts for several years.

Serious interest in Cuba did not surface again until 1868, when a rebellion broke out on the island. The Cubans, who had suffered repression at the hands of the Spanish for many years, declared independence in October and formed a shadowy provisional republican government. When Ulysses S. Grant assumed the U.S. presidency in March 1869, no one really knew how well organized the new government was or how effective its military power might be, but it soon became apparent that the rebel government had little substance and no true army. The rebels were fighting a savage hit-and-run guerrilla war. Nevertheless, rebel sympathizers in America demanded diplomatic recognition and intervention. Grant's secretary of state, Hamilton Fish, opposed such a policy on grounds that the violence in Cuba was a civil war, not a conflict between two belligerent nations. He proposed that the United States mediate the civil war and urge Spain to grant Cuba independence in exchange for an indemnity of $150 million guaranteed by the United States. Spain rejected this proposal.

President Grant disagreed with Fish. He desired to recognize Cuban belligerency as a form of revenge for Spain's recognition of Confederate belligerency during the U.S. Civil War. The president was very much under the influence of his secretary of war, John A. Rawlins, who favored intervention. In August 1869, Grant, urged on by Rawlins, ordered Fish to proclaim neutrality, which would in effect grant recognition to the Cuban rebels. Fish stalled, Rawlins soon died, and in the emotional turmoil that followed, Grant forgot about his proclamation of neutrality. Fish then persuaded the president to announce that the rebellion was not a war and that the rebels had no political organization sufficient to justify recognition.

The leaders of the Republican party in Congress did not agree with Grant and in early 1870 began to discuss the possibility of issuing a joint resolution in favor of recognition. Many newspapers, especially those in New York City, favored such a move, but Secretary Fish was alarmed because he was convinced that recognition would mean war with Spain. He urged the president to denounce the proposal and threatened to resign if he did not. Grant finally agreed and sent a message to Congress opposing the resolution. As a result the resolution failed when it came to a vote in June.

During the rebellion numerous fililbustering expeditions to Cuba originated in the United States and embarrassed the government. The most serious of these was the so-called *Virginius* affair in October 1873. A Spanish gunboat captured the *Virginius,* a rebel steamer flying the

American flag. Those aboard, including several Americans and Britons, were taken to Santiago de Cuba and tried as pirates. Fifty-three were shot, and the American government and people were outraged. Fish sent an ultimatum to the Spanish government demanding a salute to the American flag, an apology, the release of the survivors, an indemnity, and punishment of the responsible Spanish officials. By these actions Fish had taken the United States to the brink of war, but he soon discovered that his actions were hasty. He learned that the *Virginius* belonged to the Cubans, was illegally flying the U.S. flag, and was carrying arms and filibusters in violation of American law. Therefore, he dropped some of his demands. The Spanish government, which did not want war with the United States, reciprocated by releasing the prisoners and promising to pay an indemnity to the relatives of those who had been executed. Thus the crisis was averted.

But the butchery in Cuba went on, and the United States made one more attempt to stop it. In November 1875 Fish asked the Spanish government to grant the Cubans self-government. He intimated that if this were not done, the United States might be forced to intervene. Fish hoped for support from Britain and France in making this threat, but he received none. Meanwhile, the Spanish, who were weary of the bloodshed, delayed but did not reject the proposal out of hand. Finally they ended the war in 1878 by promising reform and autonomy. What followed was not real peace but a 17-year truce. In actuality there were few reforms and no autonomy, and the desire for independence in Cuba did not die.

Because the people of both Cuba and the Philippines revolted in 1895, their actions precipitated a crisis in Spain. Believing that the loss of any portion of the dwindling empire would precipitate the collapse of the already rickety monarchy, Prime Minister Antonio Cánovas del Castillo resolved to stamp out both revolts, whatever the cost. He was supported in this resolve by most politicians; the military; and, of course, the queen regent, Maria Cristina. This fateful decision was to lead to war with the United States and the loss of almost all that remained of Spain's overseas holdings.

In the United States the Philippine revolt attracted almost no attention, but Cuba was another matter. By 1895 American businessmen had built up substantial interests there, so any form of instability concerned the U.S. government. Moreover, the military operations during the revolt were conducted with great savagery on both sides and attracted public notice. The war was reported in the United States by big-city newspapers, notably the *New York World* and the *New York Journal,* whose publishers saw the conflict as an opportunity to increase circulation. Hence, their reports were highly sensational and often exaggerated. Because the papers emphasized the brutality of the Spaniards much more than that of the Cubans, American public opinion tended to favor the revolutionaries. Men like William Randolph Hearst, publisher of the *New York Journal,* cared not about accuracy, but only about profits. He told one of his artists, Frederick Remington, that if Remington would furnish the pictures, Hearst would furnish the war.

Despite the savagery of the conflict, the Spaniards soon found that they could not prevail using conventional methods because the Cubans chose to fight a guerrilla war just as they had done in the past. Finally, in February 1896, the Spanish government sent General Valeriano Weyler y Nicolau to Cuba with orders to do whatever was necessary to quell the insurrection. Weyler chose a policy known as reconcentration, which meant that he would force entire populations in certain areas to leave their homes and move to concentration camps, where they could be supervised by the Spanish armed forces. Weyler hoped this policy would lead to the collapse of the revolt in a short time, but instead it was a miserable failure. Not only did the guerrilla fighters continue their efforts, but thousands of innocent people died in the camps as well. Descriptions in the American media of these horrors led to an escalation of U.S. public outrage.

When the revolt began, Grover Cleveland, who was now president, opposed U.S. involvement, and when Congress overwhelmingly passed a resolution proposing that the United States grant belligerent status to the rebels and attempt to persuade Spain to recognize Cuban independence, he ignored it. But his days in office were numbered. The Democratic party did not even renominate him because of dissatisfaction with some of his domestic policies, and Republican William McKinley succeeded him in the election of 1896. One plank in the Republican platform had called upon the incoming president to use his influence to restore peace in Cuba and demand independence for the island, but in the early days of his administration McKinley proceeded with caution. He protested Spanish brutality but proposed no action except to offer to mediate the conflict, a policy that could not possibly succeed. The new prime minister in Spain, Práxedes Mateo Sagasta, who succeeded Cánovas in 1897, knew that independence was out of the question, whereas the leaders of the insurrection, notably General Máximo Gómez, would settle for nothing less. Gómez had come to believe that by continuing to exert massive pressure on the Spaniards by means of his guerrilla actions, the enemy would eventually tire and give up, or the Americans would intervene. Either way, he would win.

McKinley sent Stewart Woodford to Spain as his personal representative in June 1897 and continued to hope for a negotiated settlement, but these expectations were dashed by two events in February 1898. The first of these was the so-called de Lôme letter. Enrique Dupuy de Lôme was the Spanish minister to the United States. He had been in Washington since 1892, was thoroughly familiar with the American political scene, and did not trust McKinley. The minister knew that many American politicians desired a much more aggressive policy than the one McKinley favored, and he feared that the president would eventually give in to the pressure. De Lôme articulated his fears in a letter to his friend José Canalejas, who was in Washington in December 1897. The letter was stolen from Canalejas and eventually found its way into the hands of William Randolph Hearst, who published it on February 9, 1898. The American people were outraged when they read it.

The second event, which occurred just a few days later, was the sinking of the battleship *Maine*. Late in January, McKinley decided to send an American warship to Havana. Although portrayed as a "friendly gesture," this move was actually designed to signal Spain that the United States intended to protect its interests if necessary. Under the command of Captain Charles D. Sigsbee, the *Maine* steamed into the harbor at Havana on January 25, 1898. There she sat for three uneventful weeks until the night of February 15, when she suddenly blew up, killing 266 members of her crew. Although the cause of the blast has never been determined with certainty, it was in all likelihood the result of some internal malfunction. In any case, the media blamed Spain, calling the disaster an act of sabotage, and public outrage escalated. Now the pressure on the president became too intense to resist.

Realizing that war was now a distinct possibility, Congress passed a law appropriating $50 million from the treasury surplus for national defense. The funds were to be used at the president's discretion. On

April 11, McKinley asked Congress for authority to use military force to end hostilities in Cuba, and on April 19, Congress, by joint resolution, authorized American intervention to expel the Spaniards and ensure the independence of Cuba. An amendment to this resolution introduced by Senator Henry Moore Teller of Colorado disclaimed any intention to annex the island. Spain then declared war on the United States, and Congress reciprocated on April 25.

What began as an effort to stop inhuman behavior in Cuba had now erupted into a war that would be fought across half the globe, from the Philippines in the far Pacific to the Caribbean Sea. But what would be the military and naval strategy of this war, and what were its goals? These questions remained unanswered in April 1898, and the answers would emerge only gradually over the succeeding months according to a policy that featured many false starts and changes of direction.

The combatants in this war could not have been more different. Spain was a small, backward nation with a population of around 18 million, whereas the United States was a vibrant, growing giant with a population exceeding 75 million and increasing every year. The American industrial economy had also shown exceptional growth since the end of the Civil War, despite periodic recessions, whereas the Spanish economy was largely undeveloped by modern standards. To be sure, the Spanish army was much larger than the American force. Spain had 150,000 men in Cuba, 8,000 in Puerto Rico, 20,000 in the Philippines, and 150,000 at home, but they were poorly led; poorly trained; and, for the most part, poorly equipped. Moreover, many of those in the tropics suffered from debilitating illnesses. The U.S. forces consisted of 28,000 officers and men in the regular army and an additional 114,000 state militia units. The regulars were generally well trained and had many years of experience in fighting the Indians but were utterly unprepared to fight a war on a large scale. As far as the two navies were concerned, there was no comparison. America had five modern battleships, more than thirty cruisers, and many smaller vessels, whereas the ships of the Spanish navy were for the most part antique and decrepit.

It was clear from the outset that the United States could not fight an all-out war with an army of 28,000 men even if the enemy force was vastly inferior. Nevertheless, General Nelson A. Miles, commander-in-chief of the army, did not favor a call for volunteers. His initial plan was to have the navy blockade Cuba and then send in a small regular force after the Spaniards had been reduced to near starvation. He seemed to overlook the effect this plan might have on the Cubans themselves. Both the president and the secretary of war, Russell A. Alger, approved the plan until they encountered opposition from the state militias, who represented a potent political force. Because the militiamen, or National Guard, demanded to be involved and could not be ignored, in April and May McKinley called for 200,000 volunteers and at the same time requested authorization to increase the size of the regular army to 65,000. As a result, the United States had more than 290,000 men under arms before the end of the summer.

Raising such a large army in such a short time inevitably generated problems with supplies. As soon as the units were mustered they were sent to camps in various southern cities, where they were to be trained and equipped for combat. Unfortunately, the War Department simply could not handle the demand, and the result was chaos. The men were given antiquated weapons, if they were given weapons at all; they were issued uniforms designed for use in the winter; and their rations were often inedible and occasionally so spoiled as to be lethal.

Because all the men who would eventually fight in Cuba were trained in and would depart from Tampa, Florida, Tampa was where most of the logistical nightmares occurred. This city of 26,000 on the Gulf of Mexico was selected as the port of debarkation because it had shipping facilities and was the closest available site to Cuba, but its shortcomings outweighed its advantages. Only two railroads reached the city from the north and only one connected Tampa proper to Port Tampa nine miles to the south. All supplies had to be transported to Tampa by rail and then unloaded and reloaded to be taken to the port facilities. There they had to be unloaded again and reloaded on the transports that would take them to Cuba. These conditions caused a severe bottleneck. Although tons of supplies eventually arrived, they often did not find their way to their intended recipients but were seized by other units.

Presiding over the men in Tampa was the commanding general of the Fifth Army, William R. Shafter. Now close to the end of a long military career, Shafter had served with distinction in the Civil War and fought against the Plains Indians, but he had never led large groups of men in combat. Moreover, he had seen no action for years; was in poor health; and had gained considerable weight, tipping the scales at more than 300 pounds. But Shafter was at first not particularly worried about his task. He thought his objective was merely to take supplies to the rebels.

At the beginning of the war neither Shafter nor any other person in a command position knew what he was supposed to do. The navy men were not bothered much by these problems. They simply assumed that they would seek out and destroy Spanish naval forces; harass Spanish commerce; and, of course, attack Spain, and planned accordingly. The army faced a more difficult situation. Not knowing if their mission was simply to assist the rebels in Cuba or to conquer the entire Spanish empire made planning a problem. Until President McKinley made up his mind and issued a specific list of objectives, the problems would continue to befuddle the military planners.

The command structure necessary to guide the nation through this war did not exist at the outset of the crisis. It evolved during the spring of 1898. At the top, of course, was the president, who surrounded himself with numerous advisers, some of whom he relied on heavily and others whom he practically ignored. McKinley set up a war room in the White House where he met daily with his advisers. These included Secretary of the Navy John D. Long, Secretary of War Russell A. Alger, General Miles, and several others. McKinley had confidence in the abilities of Long, but he soon concluded that neither Alger nor Miles was adequate. Because McKinley himself possessed little strength of character and tended to agree with the last person he talked to, policy waffled as events unfolded.

As it turned out, the first action in the war took place not in Cuba, where the crisis had begun, but in the far-off Philippines, and the results of this action affected the direction of the war from then on. The navy's plan was to blockade Cuba and attack the Spanish squadron in the Philippines when the occasion should arise. One of the planners was Theodore Roosevelt, who in 1898 was assistant secretary of the navy. He believed that American military policy should be very aggressive; as a result, in February, without authorization, he ordered Commodore George Dewey, commander of the American Asiatic squadron, to proceed to Hong Kong and prepare to attack Manila at once in the event of war. Dewey obeyed, and Secretary Long, when he learned of Roosevelt's order, allowed it to stand.

On April 26, when Dewey received word that war had been declared, he set sail for Manila. Arriving on April 30, he discovered that the Spanish squadron, under the command of Admiral Patricio Montojo, was anchored in Manila Bay near Cavite. Dewey boldly entered the bay early on the morning of May 1 and launched his attack. Within a few hours he had inflicted a catastrophic defeat on the Spaniards and demonstrated that Spanish naval forces were no match for the Americans. This realization was to have a profound effect on policy making in Washington. Meanwhile, although his victory at sea was complete, Dewey faced a problem: he lacked sufficient forces to attack the Spanish defenses in Manila. Therefore, he cabled Washington requesting support and assisted exiled Filipino rebel leader Emilio Aguinaldo to return home from Hong Kong to rally his forces. Aguinaldo mistakenly believed that the United States intended to support his independence movement. When he later discovered otherwise, he was infuriated and turned on his erstwhile benefactors.

Meanwhile, the North Atlantic Squadron under the command of Admiral William T. Sampson had set up a blockade of Cuba according to the original plan. But about the same time that Dewey was approaching Manila, the Americans discovered that another Spanish fleet under the command of Admiral Pascual Cervera y Topete had been dispatched from Spain and was heading west. Because at first the Americans had no idea where Cervera was going or what his mission might be, he caused considerable worry. American naval forces went looking for him but somehow he escaped detection, and on May 19 he entered the harbor at Santiago on the southern coast of Cuba. Already encouraged by Dewey's victory to be more aggressive, the American planners were driven by Cervera's presence to change their plans for Cuba entirely.

The original plan to use land forces in small numbers to support the insurrection had soon given way to a much more elaborate plan to land a large army in northern Cuba and attack the Spanish garrison at Havana. That plan was now abandoned in favor of an assault on Santiago. When Admiral Sampson's squadron was joined by another under the command of Commodore Winfield Scott Schley, they trapped Cervera in Santiago Bay. Now it was decided that Schafter's army would land in the south and would attack the defenders of Santiago. The leaders hoped that when the Spaniards found themselves caught between overwhelming forces on land and sea, they would quickly give up.

When Shafter received his orders on May 31 he was still coping with severe logistical problems, which turned into a nightmare. Shafter had to coordinate the movement of 25,000 men, their equipment, and their livestock from the encampment at Tampa to Port Tampa, nine miles away. It was a difficult problem and sheer chaos ensued, but somehow all the obstacles were overcome, and the expedition was loaded and ready to sail on June 8. But before it could depart, the War Department postponed the invasion because of erroneous reports that Spanish warships were lurking in the area. The troops were required to stay on board the hot, stuffy, overcrowded transports for a week before they were finally allowed to depart on June 14.

Even as he sailed toward his objective, General Shafter did not know exactly what he was going to do. His orders gave him considerable flexibility, and it was left to him to decide precisely how to mount his assault on Santiago and in what way, if at all, he would cooperate with the navy. Before he arrived Shafter did not know that Admiral Sampson was expecting him to attack the shore batteries near the mouth of the harbor so that he could enter and engage Cervera's fleet. When he arrived, Shafter conferred with Sampson, examined his options, and made his decision. He rejected Sampson's proposal and instead undertook a landing at Daiquirí, located some thirty miles east of Santiago. From there he intended to seize the high ground north and east of the city, bombard both the city and the harbor, and force Cervera to flee his safe haven and run into the hands of the waiting Americans. Sampson did not like the plan, but there was nothing he could do about it. The landing operation was difficult and took four days, but eventually all of Shafter's forces were ashore and he was ready to proceed. He wanted to bring the mission to a conclusion as soon as possible because he feared an outbreak of disease among his troops. This fear was justified, and before the operation was complete more men died of yellow fever and other maladies than from the results of combat.

Between June 26 and July 1 the Fifth Corps fought several skirmishes. On July 1, they assaulted the village of El Caney, hoping to take it and then proceed up the heights north of the city known as San Juan Hill. After securing the heights they would be able to take the city with ease. As often occurs in combat, however, the plan did not work. Spanish resistance was fierce, and by the time the Americans had secured the village and the heights, it was too late in the day to go on. Taking advantage of the lull, the Spanish defenders retreated to a new defense line on the outskirts of the city.

Theodore Roosevelt, now a colonel leading a volunteer detachment of dismounted calvary, was shocked at the savagery of the fight and the persistence of the Spaniards. General Shafter was also concerned. He did not know how badly battered the Spaniards were and, fearing unacceptable casualties, was reluctant to launch a second assault. To make matters worse, his men were falling ill in alarming numbers. Shafter sent word to Sampson asking for a coordinated attack, but Sampson hesitated. The two commanders exchanged several communications and then planned a face-to-face conference on the morning of July 3.

Unknown to either Shafter or Sampson, Admiral Cervera had already received orders to leave the harbor and either give battle to the Americans or escape to the open sea. The honor of Spain was at stake, he was told. Cervera regarded the order as madness, but like a good soldier he obeyed. His plan was to leave on the morning of July 3, a Sunday, hoping to take the Americans by surprise. Indeed, the American commanders were surprised, but they quickly rallied and destroyed Cervera's entire fleet in a little over an hour.

Heartened by this development, Shafter demanded that General José Toral, commanding the defenders of Santiago, surrender his forces. Toral delayed, apparently hoping for some kind of miracle, but none appeared; on July 17, he laid down his arms. Shortly after that, General Miles, who had just arrived in Cuba, was authorized to lead an expedition to Puerto Rico. He left Cuba on July 21 with 3,400 men. After he arrived he was reinforced with 10,000 additional troops. They fought a few skirmishes as they moved toward San Juan, but hostilities ended before they could assault the capital.

While these events unfolded in the Caribbean, Dewey awaited his reinforcements in Manila Bay. McKinley soon authorized a 20,000-man expedition designated as the Eighth Corps and placed General Wesley Merritt in command. When Merritt asked the president precisely what the goals of his mission would be, the president equivocated. Thus Merritt set out on this peculiar operation not knowing if he should merely capture Manila or attempt to conquer the entire Philippine archipelago. He departed on May 25 and arrived in Manila Bay on June 30.

There was at least one specific element in Merritt's orders: he was not to cooperate in any way with Aguinaldo, whose force of approximately 12,000 men already had Manila surrounded. By this time

Aguinaldo had proclaimed independence and named himself dictator. He did not intend to be simply pushed aside by the Americans. Merritt positioned his forces behind the Filipinos and began to consider his options, but before he could act, the Spanish commander, Fermín Jáudenes, realizing that his position was hopeless, asked for a parley. He was terrified of falling into the hands of the Filipinos and offered to surrender to the Americans provided they would participate in a sham battle in order to preserve Spanish honor. Merritt agreed, and on August 13 the charade was played out. The Americans advanced through Filipino lines with the reluctant consent of Aguinaldo, exchanged a few shots with the enemy, then entered the city and accepted its surrender. Unknown to Merritt, Jáudenes, or Aguinaldo, the United States and Spain had agreed to an armistice two days earlier.

After the debacle in Cuba, the Spanish government concluded that to continue would be madness, and they asked the French to transmit a request for a cease-fire to the Americans. McKinley accepted the offer on August 12 on the condition that Spain give up control of Cuba, cede Puerto Rico to the United States, and also turn over control of an island in the Pacific. The Philippine question was to be resolved at a peace conference to be held in Paris. Although McKinley had still not decided what to do about the Philippines, he really had little choice. Expansionist sentiment was escalating daily and could not be ignored. Moreover, it was obvious that the islands could not be allowed to fall into the hands of another power, and hardly anyone believed that the Filipinos were ready to govern themselves. At length McKinley authorized his representatives to demand cession of the Philippines in exchange for a cash settlement. After some delay the Spanish commissioners agreed, and the Treaty of Paris was signed on December 10, 1898.

Aguinaldo was enraged when he heard of these developments and refused to concede. On February 4, 1899, fighting erupted between his forces and those of the Eighth Corps, now under the command of General Elwell S. Otis. This was the beginning of another war—a war that would be longer, bloodier, and infinitely more savage than the war with Spain. It would last until 1902 and was known as the Philippine Insurrection. To put down this rebellion it became necessary to increase American military power, and by 1900 well over 70,000 troops were in the Philippines. They faced an enemy force of almost 50,000 scattered about the islands. Most of the fighting took place on the island of

Luzon, where at first the Filipinos engaged in conventional warfare. Such a strategy was a recipe for disaster, and by the autumn of 1899 they appeared to have been defeated. The Americans soon learned, however, that the war was not over. Aguinaldo had merely withdrawn into the hills and shifted to a strategy of guerrilla warfare similar to that used by the Cubans. In this way he was able to fight on for another two years. During this time each side became enraged with the barbarity of the other, and there were many atrocities. The struggle was finally brought to an end by General Arthur MacArthur, who replaced Otis in 1900. He established garrisons at strategically important locations throughout the islands and set out to harass the guerrillas to the point of exhaustion. This strategy was successful, and the guerrilla bands began to disperse. Aguinaldo himself was captured in October 1901. He issued a proclamation calling for peace, and the Americans reciprocated in July 1902. President Roosevelt granted amnesty to the rebels at the same time. The American wars of expansion were now over. The era of their consequences was just beginning.[1]

Note

1. For further reading, see T. Harry Williams, *The History of American Wars* (New York: Knopf, 1981); Elbert J. Benton, *International Law and Diplomacy of the Spanish-American War* (Baltimore: Johns Hopkins, 1908); H. W. Brands, *The Reckless Decade: Americans in the 1890s* (New York: St. Martin's Press, 1995); and Louis A. Perez, *Cuba and the United States: Ties of Singular Intimacy* (Athens: University of Georgia Press, 1990).

CHAPTER 2

THE ORIGINS OF THE WAR

The United States went to war with Spain in 1898 because of a series of events that took place in Cuba. Neither side wanted war, but the two nations were inexorably drawn to it by an accumulation of circumstances that seemed to take on a life of their own. The process began on February 25, 1895, with the outbreak of a revolt against Spanish authority in eastern Cuba. The Cubans had never been content under Spanish rule and had risen up before (1868–1878) without success. This time violence was triggered by economic desperation caused by a sudden decline in American demand for Cuban sugar, a decline attributed to the Dingley Tariff of 1894, which placed an import tax of 40 percent on imported sugar. As a result of this decline, the living conditions of ordinary Cubans, already low, became intolerable.

The leaders of the Cuban revolt of 1895 included José Martí, who had devoted most of his adult life to the cause of independence, along with Máximo Gómez and Antonio Maceo, who had fought in previous uprisings. Their strategy was simple and brutal. They intended to carry out a scorched-earth campaign that would make the cost of maintaining control so great that Spain would have no alternative but to yield. Their goal was independence, and from the outset they determined that they would settle for nothing less. In the early stages of the revolt the rebels established a committee, or *junta,* in New York City to promote their cause and conduct propaganda activities in the United States. They also set up a revolutionary government representing the Republic of Cuba. Martí was killed early in the fighting and Gómez emerged as the leader. He and his followers believed the United States would intervene in the war for both humanitarian and economic reasons and victory would be inevitable.[1]

In Spain the Conservative party, led by Antonio Cánovas del Castillo, was in power. Cánovas was prepared to take whatever steps might be necessary to preserve Spanish control over Cuba. He believed that to lose Cuba or even to compromise in any way with the rebels would bring down his government and perhaps even the monarchy. To forestall such a calamity Cánovas sent General Valeriano Weyler y Nicolau to Cuba to put down the rebellion. Weyler took command on February 10, 1896, and immediately inaugurated a policy of "reconcentration." Under this policy the inhabitants of certain areas were moved to new locations—essentially concentration camps—near military headquarters, where they would be less able to aid the revolutionaries. Weyler believed that his policy would bring a quick end to the war because it would deny the insurgents access to essential supplies and replacements. Overcrowding and unsanitary conditions led to great suffering for hundreds of thousands of people and resulted in the deaths of at least one hundred thousand. It also triggered outrage in the United States, which in turn caused the Spanish government to fear the possibility of American intervention. But Weyler assured Cánovas that he would achieve pacification by early 1898—long before the Americans could act.[2]

Weyler's confidence was entirely misplaced. The reconcentration policy failed to produce the desired results in Cuba, and the outcry of rage in the United States, exacerbated by lurid newspaper accounts, brought public opinion to the boiling point much more quickly than expected. Meanwhile, President Grover Cleveland held steadfastly to a policy of neutrality. He did not want to recognize the Cuban revolutionary government, nor did he want to consider intervention. He also understood that Cánovas was trying to generate support for Spain's position in practically all the capitals of Europe, and this was cause for concern. At the same time he recognized that Weyler's activities had caused an emotional upheaval at home that could not be quelled. Thus he left office a worried man.[3]

William McKinley took office as president in March 1897, knowing that emotions were running high but hoping that he could avoid a conflict. His primary goal was to end the depression at home—a major economic disaster that had started in 1893. He also knew that Spain desired peace, and he was somewhat relieved when Cánovas announced the inauguration of reform in April 1897. Under these circumstances McKinley decided to send a new minister to Spain with instructions to find grounds for a reasonable settlement that would avoid war. He appointed Stewart L. Woodford, a well-known New York lawyer. Prior to Woodford's' departure for Madrid, McKinley revealed his negotiating position to the Spanish minister, Enrique Dupuy de Lôme, who relayed the terms to his superiors. McKinley wanted Weyler's reconcentration policy terminated, hostilities ended, relief provided to those in need, and a permanent change made in the Spanish-Cuban relationship. By this he is assumed to have meant home rule. He was disappointed when he learned that the Spanish leaders did not intend to change their current policies.[4]

Things changed dramatically on August 8, 1897, when Cánovas was assassinated and the Queen Regent replaced him with the liberal Práxedes Mateo Sagasta. Sagasta was no more willing than any other Spanish leader to give up Cuba, but he was willing to be much more flexible in dealing with the rebels and the Americans. He recalled Weyler at once and in the fall of 1897 announced that his government would grant autonomy to Cuba. He also made it clear that he wanted American support in his efforts to pacify the island. Unfortunately, Sagasta's plan could not possibly succeed. The rebels, now more determined than ever to gain independence, believed that continuation of the struggle would soon force the United States to intervene. Stewart Woodford, observing these events closely, concluded that Spain sincerely wanted to avoid war but that it might be impossible: "The insurrection may have acquired such strength that nothing short of complete independence will induce the insurgents to lay down their arms," he wrote.[5]

By the end of 1897, although peace had not been restored, war between the United States and Spain was not inevitable. Almost certainly, the Cubans desired American intervention, but conditions had not yet spiraled so far out of control as to precipitate such action. In early 1898, however, two events occurred in rapid succession that triggered a crisis. One was the unauthorized publication of a letter written by the Spanish minister, Enrique Dupuy de Lôme, that was critical of President McKinley, and the other was the destruction of the battleship *Maine* in Havana's harbor. Reaction to these events in the United States led directly to war.

On February 9, 1898, the *New York Journal* published a private letter from Dupuy de Lôme to José Canalejas, a Spanish journalist who
had been visiting in Washington in December 1897. Canalejas took the
letter with him when he returned to Havana, where it was stolen. The
thief brought the document back to the United States and gave it to
Tomás Estrada Palma, head of the Cuban junta in New York. Estrada
then ensured that the letter was delivered to William Randolph Hearst,
publisher of the *Journal*. When Dupuy de Lôme learned what had happened, he resigned on February 8, and the letter was published the following day. In the letter Dupuy de Lôme discussed the political climate
in Washington, said he opposed negotiations with the rebels, and
referred to the president as a "weak bidder for the admiration of the
crowd . . . " (and) . . . "a would-be politician, who tries to leave the
door open behind himself while keeping on good terms with the jingoes of his party."[6]

Of course, the publication of the letter generated outrage, but this
uproar was nothing compared to that triggered by the events of the following week. On the night of February 15, 1898, the battleship *Maine*
suddenly blew up at her mooring in the harbor at Havana, killing 266
members of her crew. President McKinley had dispatched the ship to
Cuba late in January on a "mission of friendship," which was really a
thinly disguised signal to Spain that he was prepared to defend American citizens and interests in Cuba if necessary. The vessel, which
arrived on January 25, remained in the harbor for an uneventful three
weeks. Captain Charles D. Sigsbee and his officers went ashore on
numerous occasions to dine, attend the bullfights, and socialize with
Spanish officials. On the night of the explosion the captain was in his
quarters writing a letter to his wife in which he remarked on how
peaceful the sojourn had been.[7]

The day after the sinking, newspapers all over the United States
carried stories describing the tragedy and suggesting that the Spanish
authorities were responsible. Spain, of course, denied any involvement. Subsequently, two separate commissions investigated the blast
and produced contradictory reports. The American commission concluded that the source of the explosion was external and the result of
sabotage. The Spanish commission concluded that the source was
internal and the sinking was thus a horrible accident.[8] An objective
evaluation of the reports forces one to conclude that the Spanish docu-

ment is the more persuasive of the two, but at the time it was of no consequence. American public opinion blamed Spain and demanded revenge.

Although some prominent Americans such as Edwin L. Godkin, publisher of the influential journal *The Nation,* deplored the idea of a war of vengeance, the public demanded action and placed President McKinley in a difficult position. He did not want war, but at the same time he could not ignore the growing pressure. Therefore, he sent instructions to Woodford telling him to persuade the Spanish government to do whatever was necessary to make Cuban autonomy a reality. Sagasta, however, had already decided on a policy of delay. His position was difficult, too. On the one hand, he feared that making too many concessions might weaken or topple his government, but on the other, he realized that the Americans would soon lose patience.[9]

Meanwhile, McKinley prepared for the war he hoped to avoid. He pushed a $50 million defense appropriation through Congress during the first week of March. The vote was unanimous in both houses. The Spanish government viewed the move as a signal that the Americans were serious, whereas the Cuban rebels saw it as a sign that perseverance would ensure ultimate victory. Thus any hope for the success of the autonomy policy was now gone. A sequence of events had been generated that would soon swirl out of control.[10]

On March 17, 1898, Senator Redfield Proctor (R-Vermont) rose to address his colleagues. He had recently returned from a tour of Cuba and described what he had seen. Because Proctor was highly respected by conservatives and the business community his views were taken seriously. His remarks intensified the demand for intervention, even though Proctor claimed it was not his intention to promote war. In part, the senator said,[11]

> I went to Cuba with a strong conviction that the situation had been overdrawn. I could not believe that out of a population of 1,600,000, two hundred thousand had died within these Spanish forts. . . . What I saw I cannot tell so that others can see it. It must be seen with one's own eyes to be realized. . . . To me the strongest appeal is not the barbarity practiced by Weyler, nor the loss of the *Maine* . . . but the spectacle of a million and a half people, the entire native population of Cuba struggling for freedom and deliverance from the worst misgovernment of which I ever had knowledge.

Events now moved quickly. On March 27 Woodford was instructed to explain clearly the American position to the Spanish government. The Americans wanted an end to reconcentration, an immediate armistice, and a commitment by Spain to accept Cuban independence. These demands were essentially an ultimatum and meant that the relationship between the United States and Spain had passed the point of no return. Because the Spanish government refused to grant independence for Cuba, war was now inevitable.[12]

In one last, desperate effort to avoid conflict the Spanish government sought support from the great powers of Europe, but none was forthcoming. Though European leaders claimed to sympathize with Spain, they had no desire to antagonize the United States. In any case, they had more important matters to attend to in their own overseas empires. The Vatican made known its willingness to mediate the dispute, but McKinley rejected this offer. At this point the Spanish made the last move available to them—they accepted the American ultimatum in part. They proclaimed an armistice and announced termination of the reconcentration system. Unfortunately, the armistice period was shorter than what the Americans demanded and there was no mention of independence. Hence this move was unacceptable to the Americans, and of course, it meant nothing to the Cubans, who were committed to independence.[13]

On April 11, 1898, President McKinley asked Congress for authority to intervene in Cuba, believing that he could no longer resist the pressures being generated by public opinion and the proponents of war in his own party. Like everyone else, McKinley knew American intervention would lead to Cuban independence, but he did not offer recognition to the provisional government of the Cuban Republic because he believed that such an action would limit his options. His message concluded with the following stirring words:

> In the name of humanity, in the name of civilization, on behalf of endangered American interests which give us the right and the duty to speak and act, the war in Cuba must stop. . . . I ask Congress to authorize and empower the President to take measures to secure the full and final termination of hostilities between the government of Spain and the people of Cuba, and to recover in the island the establishment of a stable government . . . and to use the military and naval forces of the United States as may be necessary for these purposes. . . . I have exhausted every effort to relieve the

intolerable condition of affairs which is at our door. Prepared to execute every obligation imposed upon me by the Constitution and the law, I await your action.[14]

McKinley's message generated considerable debate in Congress because many members favored granting diplomatic recognition to the Cuban Republic, but the debate was resolved with the introduction of an amendment by Senator Henry M. Teller (R-Colorado) disclaiming any intention by the United States to annex Cuba. This proposal supported the claim that the Americans were going to war on humanitarian grounds and led to the passage on April 19 of a joint resolution favoring intervention. McKinley signed the measure the following day. Spain, now out of options, declared war on April 23, and the United States reciprocated on April 25. However, because the navy had been ordered to blockade the northern coast of Cuba on April 21, the American declaration was made retroactive to that date.[15]

Because it was always assumed in Spain that a diplomatic solution to the crisis would be achieved, there had been practically no preparations for war. The Spanish navy was in poor condition and Spanish ground forces in Cuba and the Philippines were inadequately supplied. Nevertheless, once the declarations of war were issued, some effort was required to prepare for action. Admiral Pascual Cervera y Topete, commander of the naval squadron at Cádiz, was ordered to get ready to defend Spanish waters and to fight the Americans in the Caribbean.[16] Because of the condition of his resources, Cervera regarded his mission as impossible and protested to his superiors while at the same time moving ahead loyally to do his duty. Cervera wrote,[17]

> Do we not owe to our country not only our life, if necessary but the exposition of our beliefs? I am very uneasy about this. I ask myself if it is right . . . to make myself an accomplice in an adventure which will surely cause the total ruin of Spain. And for what purpose? To defend an island which was ours, but belongs to us no more because even if we did not lose it by right in war we have lost it in fact, and with it all our wealth and an enormous number of young men . . . in the defense of what is now no more than a romantic idea.

At the same time Spanish authorities in the Philippines knew they would be attacked by American naval forces under the command of

Commodore George Dewey. They also knew that they had little hope of successfully defending the islands because of the superiority of Dewey's forces. Admiral Patricio Montojo, commander of the naval squadron at Manila, did what he could to prepare and called desperately for reinforcements, which were not forthcoming. Spain's navy was not large enough to dispatch Cervera to the Caribbean, defend Spanish waters, and assist Montojo all at the same time.

Before the sinking of the *Maine,* the United States had made no comprehensive plans for war, but after February 15, planning suddenly went forward at a feverish pace. This activity was based on general discussions of possible naval and military scenarios developed earlier by the War Department. These scenarios assumed that war with Spain would entail blockades of Cuba and Puerto Rico, a land operation in Cuba, an attack on Manila, and possible naval operations in Spanish waters. It was also assumed that the navy would bear most of the operational burden.

The quickening of American preparations began on February 25, when the assistant secretary of the navy, Theodore Roosevelt, sent his famous message to Commodore George Dewey ordering him to prepare to attack Manila in the event of war. Dewey proceeded to prepare for the operation. A few days later the secretary of the navy, John D. Long, ordered the battleship *Oregon* to begin the long voyage from the Pacific to the Caribbean. At about the same time the navy began to purchase ships from other countries and to add personnel. By the middle of March Navy Department officials were beginning to discuss the disposition of forces. A new squadron was formed at Hampton Roads, Virginia. Known as the Flying Squadron, its initial mission was to defend the East Coast. Another battle group was formed in Florida whose mission it would be to impose a blockade on Cuba at the appropriate time.

In addition to these operational plans, Secretary Long also organized a group, which came to be known as the Naval War Board, to provide advice. At first, this group included Theodore Roosevelt; Captain Arent S. Crowninshield, chief of the Bureau of Navigation; and two other officers. Roosevelt soon departed and was replaced by Admiral Alfred Thayer Mahan.[18] Thus the U.S. navy was ready for action before the end of April 1898. The army, however, was not. Mobilization of ground forces did not begin until after hostilities began in April.

Notes

1. David Trask, *The War with Spain in 1898* (New York: Macmillan, 1981), pp. 1–6.

2. John L. Offner, *An Unwanted War: The Diplomacy of the United States and Spain Over Cuba, 1895–1898* (Chapel Hill: University of North Carolina Press, 1992), pp. 12–14.

3. Robert McElroy, *Grover Cleveland: The Man and the Statesman* (New York: Harper and Brothers, 1923), pp. 245–55.

4. Margaret Leech, *In the Days of McKinley* (New York: Harper and Brothers, 1959), pp. 148–50.

5. Trask, *The War with Spain in 1898*, p. 19.

6. ————., p. 28.

7. For a thorough discussion of the *Maine* disaster see Peggy and Harold Samuels, *Remembering the Maine* (Washington, D.C.: Smithsonian Institution Press, 1995).

8. For partial text of the two reports see Charles D. Sigsbee, *The Maine, an Account of her Destruction in Havana Harbor: Personal Narrative* (New York: Century, 1899), pp. 207–12, 231–45.

9. Trask, *The War with Spain in 1898*, p. 26.

10. Walter Millis, *The Martial Spirit* (Boston: Haughton-Miflin, 1931), pp. 115–18.

11. *Congressional Record,* 55th Cong., 2d sess., March 17, 1898, pp. 2916–19.

12. George J. A. O'Toole, *The Spanish War—An American Epic—1898* (New York: W. W. Norton, 1984), p. 160.

13. Trask, *The War with Spain in 1898,* pp. 15–51.

14. O'Toole, *The Spanish War—An American Epic—1898,* pp. 169–70.

15. For a discussion of the debate see Offner, *An Unwanted War,* pp. 188–93; for a discussion of the decision of the Spanish government to accept war see Ernest R. May, *Imperial Democracy: The Emergence of America as a Great Power* (New York: Harcourt, Brace, and World, 1961), pp. 160–77.

16. Trask, *The War with Spain in 1898,* pp. 61–68.

17. ————., pp. 63–64.

18. For a full discussion of war preparations by the U.S. navy see ibid., pp. 72–94.

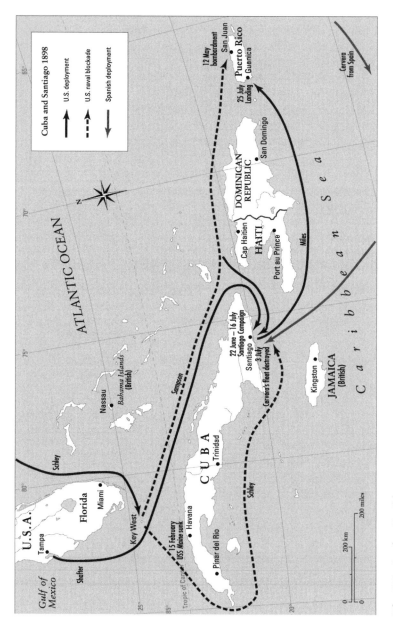

The War in the Caribbean

CHAPTER 3

CAMPAIGNING IN CUBA AND PUERTO RICO

During the months of diplomatic wrangling that preceded the outbreak of hostilities, next to nothing was done to properly prepare and equip the U.S. army. Hence the War Department needed to address numerous inadequacies before any consideration could be given to engaging Spanish forces. In April 1898, the U.S. army numbered only 28,000 officers and men scattered in small contingents all over the country. In addition, approximately 114,000 officers and men were in the various state militias. These forces, however, were poorly trained and badly equipped. Moreover, it was questionable whether the president could legally mobilize the militias for overseas service and, even if he did, if they could be used effectively.

One reason for the dallying by the War Department was that for years it had been assumed that in the event of a war with Spain the brunt of the offensive action would be borne by the navy, with the army in a largely defensive and supporting role. As the reality of war approached, however, things changed. The U.S. military planners now assumed that offensive land operations would be conducted in the Caribbean and that large numbers of men would be needed. Thus, mobilization began. Most of the regular army was moved to two locations—Camp Thomas in Tennessee and Tampa, Florida—and the president issued a call for volunteers. The War Department had expected him to call for 60,000, but the president summoned 125,000, probably hoping his action would frighten the Spanish government and induce them to settle the dispute without combat. Congress also authorized the expansion of the regular army, and the president issued a second call for volunteers—this time summoning 75,000. The response to these calls was overwhelming; before the war ended in August 1898, the size of the armed forces—army and navy—had reached nearly 290,000 men. Because the war turned out to be very brief, however, few of these men were ever committed to combat.[1]

Most of the volunteers were sent to four training sites—Camp Thomas in Tennessee; Tampa, where regular army units were already in residence; Camp Alger in Virginia; and the Presidio near San Francisco. The concentration of large numbers of men in relatively small places without adequate preparation led to serious problems, the worst of which was disease. The camps soon turned into little more than garbage dumps, and troops who resided there were miserable.[2] Meanwhile, the War Department, which had no strategic plan, set out to develop one. General William R. Shafter, placed in command of the troops at Tampa, was told to prepare for a brief expedition to Cuba, the main purpose of which would be to take supplies to General Máximo Gómez, the leader of the Cuban rebels. This plan was dropped almost at once when it was learned that Admiral Pascual Cervera was on his way to the West Indies in command of a Spanish naval squadron. The next plan called for Shafter's force to attack Havana as soon as possible, but this was also quickly dropped when General of the Army Nelson A. Miles pointed out to the president that nearly 125,000 Spanish troops were in the vicinity of Havana. No attack should be directed there, he argued, until more specific plans were developed for landing and supporting the American forces.

The arrival of Admiral Cervera's squadron at Santiago in late May triggered the emergence of a plan that was eventually followed—more or less. Any thought of attacking Havana was dropped, and it was decided to send expeditions to Santiago and Puerto Rico. The military reasoned that such a deployment would force the Spaniards to defend their territory at their weakest points, would ensure success, and would give American forces powerful bases from which to operate should the conflict turn out to take longer than expected. In fact, President McKinley wanted to inflict such heavy losses on the Spanish forces that their government would sue for peace as soon as possible, but he could not yet be certain that this strategy would succeed. At this point no serious discussions of annexation had taken place.[3]

Once McKinley and his advisers decided to attack Santiago they also decided that the main expeditionary force would embark from

Tampa. Even though General Miles was the highest-ranking officer in the army and could have assumed command, he chose to assign this responsibility to General Shafter and devote himself to preparing for the assault on Puerto Rico. This decision pleased Secretary of War Russell A. Alger, who despised Miles and hoped to keep him out of the limelight. And so it was that General William R. Shafter undertook preparations for the great adventure. Because conditions were not ideal and because Shafter was not prepared to guide such a large undertaking, the confusion and ineptitude that were commonplace at Tampa would characterize the invasion as well. The war would be won, but it was the valor of the men who fought combined with sheer luck, not leadership, that produced the result.

The troops, mostly volunteers, arrived in Tampa during May. Selected as the point of departure for the invasion of Cuba because it had shipping facilities and was the closest available port to the target, Tampa actually had little to offer. It was just a small town awash in sand. Because there were no facilities adequate to support the sudden arrival of thousands of men, it was necessary to rush in tons of supplies. Unfortunately, only two railroads reached Tampa and only one track connected the town to Port Tampa, some nine miles farther south. The result was chaos. The troops were required to set up their own camps and maintain them during their stay in Tampa. Mercifully, this sojourn was brief, or else almost certainly they would have suffered major outbreaks of disease as did the men in all the other camps where military units were kept for extended periods. The men at Tampa received very little training; even if they had, it would have been of little use because few of their officers, including General Shafter, were competent to train large groups of men for combat. To make matters worse, the supplies that did arrive were inadequate. Most of the uniforms were made of blue wool suited for service in Alaska rather than the tropics, and the weapons most of the men received were obsolete Springfield rifles that placed them at a great disadvantage when they faced the Spanish forces in combat.

Once it was learned in Washington that Admiral Cervera's squadron had arrived at Santiago, the administration became anxious for the expedition to depart quickly. Secretary Alger sent several contradictory messages to Shafter ordering him to depart before he was ready; these caused great confusion, but finally the troops, their supplies, and

their animals began loading on June 6.[4] Because the United States had
no troopships when the war began, the vessels to be used for the expedition had to be leased from private owners. This was not easy, but
eventually 38 ships were assembled—most of them dirty, run-down,
and cramped. On board almost everything was inadequate to accommodate large numbers of men. There was insufficient fresh air below
deck and not enough water for drinking, cooking, and sanitary purposes. Luckily, the voyage would be short.

Unaware of the discomfort that awaited them and impatient to
seek adventure and glory in Cuba, the troops were eager to board the
waiting vessels when the time came to depart on June 6. Competition
for space became acute when it was learned that the 38 available ships
could accommodate only about 16,000 men along with their supplies
and livestock. Because there were more than 20,000 men in Tampa and
everybody wanted to go, wagons were stolen, train cars were comman-
deered, and entire trains were hijacked—all in a mad scramble to get
from Tampa to Port Tampa in time to secure space on one or another of
the decrepit troop transports. Of course, the most famous boarding
exploit was that of Theodore Roosevelt and the Rough Riders. Roosevelt and his friend and commander Colonel Leonard Wood piled
their men on coal cars that they rode to the dock. They found their ship
but simultaneously discovered she had been assigned to two other
units.[5] Roosevelt described the chaos that followed:[6]

> At last, however, after an hour's industrious and rapid search
> through the anti-heap of humanity, Wood and I, who had sepa-
> rated, found Colonel Humphrey at nearly the same time and were
> allotted a transport—the *Yucatan*. She was out in midstream, so
> Wood seized a stray launch and boarded her. At the same time I
> happened to find out that she had been allotted to two other regi-
> ments, the Second Regular Infantry and the Seventy-First New
> York Volunteers. . . . Accordingly, I ran full speed to our train; and
> leaving a strong guard with the luggage I double-quicked the rest
> of the regiment up to the boat just in time to board her as she came
> into the quay and then to hold her against the Second Regulars and
> the Seventy-First, who had arrived a little too late . . . .

Once they were aboard, however, rumors that a Spanish naval
squadron had been sighted in the gulf caused a delay. It was a full week

before these rumors were dispelled, and during that time conditions on the overcrowded ships were appalling. Roosevelt became enraged:[7]

> The steamer on which we are contains one thousand men, there being room for about five hundred comfortably. . . . several companies are down in the lower hold, which is suggestive of the black hole of Calcutta. . . . Now, if this were necessary no one would complain for a moment. . . . But it is absolutely unnecessary; the five days of intense heat and crowded conditions are telling visibly on the spirits and health of the troops.

Finally, they set out and on June 20, 1898, after slightly more than two weeks at sea, the American convoy arrived off the southern coast of Cuba, about 30 miles east of Santiago. There followed an amphibious attack, which succeeded only because the Spanish had decided not to defend the coast in force. Had they done so losses would have been appalling. The Spanish commander in eastern Cuba, Lieutenant General Arsenio Linares Pomba, had some 24,500 men, but they were dispersed in several scattered locations. The city of Santiago, with a population of about 30,000, was defended by a force of 9,500, many of whom were sick. Linares chose not to move any of his forces, fearing that any location he evacuated would be overrun by Cuban insurgents. He had decided not to oppose the landing because positioning his men on the coast would expose them to attack from the rear, and because of the difficulty of moving artillery pieces over the hilly and heavily forested terrain. Linares's men at Santiago were under the direct command of Generals José Toral and Joaquín Vara del Rey. It would be their responsibility to repel the inevitable American assault.[8]

The Americans went ashore near the coastal village of Daiquirí. Because the water was shallow, lifeboats were lowered and the men and their supplies were slowly and laboriously rowed in while horses swam. Unaware that Linares did not intend to defend the coast, the Americans were surprised when they experienced only a few losses, all due to accidents. Writing later, the artist Frederick Remington, who witnessed the landing from one of the ships, said, "We held our breath. We expected a most desperate fight for the landing."[9]

Admiral William T. Sampson, the commander of the American naval squadron off the coast, wanted Shafter first to attack and seize the

Spanish batteries on the heights above the entrance to Santiago Bay so that he could safely enter the harbor and engage Cervera's squadron, but Shafter, determined to launch an assault against the city from the interior, refused. This incident marked the beginning of an unpleasant relationship between the general and the admiral that would last until the end of the campaign. General Shafter's decision to strike directly at Santiago stemmed primarily from his belief that he must conclude his mission quickly before tropical diseases could incapacitate his army. He was well aware of the dangers of dysentery, malaria, and yellow fever and knew that to stay too long in Cuba was to court disaster. But there was another reason for his decision that was much more personal: he did not want to share the glory of victory with the navy.[10]

Shortly after landing Shafter contacted the Cuban rebels, who, because they wanted the U.S. forces there, offered their cooperation. Several thousand men under the command of General Calixto García were assigned to four sites in the vicinity of Santiago to prevent Spanish forces from concentrating there once they realized that the city was the primary American target. At first Cuban-American relations were amiable, but they soon deteriorated. After observing them for a short time, most American fighting men concluded that the Cubans were thieves and liars and almost useless in battle. This was not entirely fair. The Cubans had acquitted themselves well on more than one occasion in battles against Spanish forces, but they soon began to suspect (correctly) that the Americans were not fighting for Cuban independence, and this realization soured their attitude.

Shafter began his advance on June 22 and easily occupied the village of Siboney the following day without engaging the enemy. But on June 24 an American unit under the command of General Joseph Wheeler saw action near the village of Las Guásimas, about three miles west of Siboney. Wheeler, who had fought bravely for the Confederacy during the Civil War, had been recruited by McKinley as a symbol. The animosity between the North and South had not entirely evaporated in the 1890s, and McKinley believed that Northern and Southern men fighting together would do much to heal old wounds. Wheeler was old, but he wanted to be much more than a symbol; he wanted to fight. Not only that, he wanted the distinction of having drawn first blood in the conflict. So he proceeded to launch an attack without orders.

Early on the morning of June 24 Wheeler sent two columns toward Las Guásimas. On the right was a brigade led by General Samuel Young and on the left were the Rough Riders commanded by Leonard Wood and Theodore Roosevelt. After a difficult march they came in view of the Spanish defenders and opened fire. The exchange lasted for about two hours, after which time the defenders executed a planned withdrawal. The Americans suffered 68 casualties—16 killed, 52 wounded—and the Spaniards lost 10 killed and 25 wounded. Wheeler and his officers, believing they had forced the enemy to flee, were exultant, and Wheeler allegedly exclaimed, "We've got the damn Yankees on the run."[11] This was reported in the newspapers at home with much good humor along with a description of the skirmish, and for a brief moment all regional and racial animosities disappeared as the public marveled at the idea of American soldiers from the North and South, black and white, routing a dastardly foe. Journalist Richard Harding Davis, who observed the assault, described the final moments of the battle:[12]

> Toward the last, the firing from the enemy sounded less near, and the bullets passed much higher. Roosevelt, who had picked up a carbine and was firing occasionally to give the direction to the others, decided on a charge. Wood, at the other end of the line, decided at the same time on the same maneuver. . . . The Spaniards naturally could not believe that this thin line . . . was the entire fighting force against it. They supposed the entire regiment was very close on its heels. . . . They fired a few parting volleys and broke and ran. . . .

In reality, the fight had been unnecessary—Las Guásimas could have been easily bypassed. But this victory boosted morale at the time and was later officially designated as the event that inspired the men to go on to victory. Wheeler was never criticized or blamed for exceeding his orders.

Immediately after the action at Las Guásimas, Shafter began planning for an assault against Santiago. Between the American forces and the city were situated several Spanish strong points, the most dangerous of which were the village of El Caney, Kettle Hill, and San Juan Heights. El Caney was on the Americans' right flank and the hills were directly between them and the city. The plan was to send one division, under

General Henry W. Lawton, against El Caney and a second, under General Henry M. Duffield, against Aguadores, a small town near the mouth of Santiago Bay. The main assault on the hills would be led by generals Joe Wheeler and Jacob Kent. It was assumed that Lawton would have little trouble taking El Caney and would join the main attack in about two hours. This plan required a frontal assault without artillery support against entrenched defenders. It was based on the assumption that the Spanish soldiers could not or would not fight effectively, but this assumption proved utterly misguided.

The engagement opened at daybreak on July 1 when Duffield began his feint toward Aguadores. His forces never got close to the enemy because a large gorge lay between them. After a brief exchange of fire from a long distance, Duffield returned to Siboney, and his effort had no effect on the outcome of the battle. Lawton attacked El Caney at about 7:00 A.M., expecting to gain control of the town by 9:00 A.M. and then move on to San Juan Heights, but it soon became clear that this was not to be. The Spanish defenders, commanded by General Joaquín Vara del Rey, numbered only around 500 and were outnumbered by the Americans 10 to 1, but they were well entrenched and put up a tenacious struggle. More than half the defenders, including General Vara del Rey, were killed or wounded, but they held off the American assault for more than eight hours. The Americans also suffered heavy casualties, with 81 killed and 360 wounded. This was another battle that probably should never have taken place. Shafter erred in ordering a frontal assault against such a strong position. Instead, the Spaniards at El Caney should have been held in place by a smaller force while Lawton was sent to engage in the main assault against San Juan Heights. The Spanish defenders there would then have been more quickly overwhelmed and Santiago might have fallen that very day.[13]

After witnessing the battle, the British military attaché, Captain Arthur H. Lee, asked someone if it was common practice for the Americans to assault blockhouses and rifle pits before they had been hit by artillery. He was told, "Not always." Later, Lee wrote:[14]

> This was a heavy price to pay for the possession of an outlying post, defended by an inferior force, but it only bore out the well-known military axiom that an attack on a fortified village cannot succeed, without great loss of life, unless the assailants are strong in

artillery. . . . that the attack succeeded was entirely due to the magnificent courage and endurance of the infantry officers and men.

According to the original plan the assault on San Juan Heights was to begin at 10:00 A.M., but it was delayed until 1:00 P.M. The delay resulted from the length of the struggle at El Caney and from mass confusion among the units moving into position. They encountered difficult, heavily overgrown terrain and were subjected to withering fire from the Spanish defenders above them. By around noon several thousand American infantrymen found themselves at the base of the hill unprotected by supporting artillery fire. Realizing that the men had been maneuvered into an untenable position, Lieutenant John D. Miley, Shafter's aide, on his own responsibility ordered a charge. It was either that or retreat. Miley made the right choice.

What followed was the main engagement of the war in Cuba. It was brief but very bloody. On the American left a brigade led by General Hamilton S. Hawkins moved up San Juan Hill. As they did so a machine gun detachment under Lieutenant John H. Parker directed a covering fire at the Spanish defenders atop the hill. This fire lasted only about eight minutes, but it drove the defenders back, and the Americans were soon in control.

Meanwhile, dismounted cavalry, including the First Volunteer Cavalry led by Theodore Roosevelt, stormed up nearby Kettle Hill. As in the case of San Juan Hill, the Spanish defenders inflicted heavy casualties upon the attackers and then withdrew to establish a defensive perimeter on the outskirts of the city about two miles to the west. Before night fell the Americans controlled all of San Juan Heights, but they were exhausted and did not press a further attack against the city. Thus ended the fighting in Cuba. A standoff ensued for the next two weeks until the Spanish surrendered.[15] The war would be won, but some of the participants thought something more important had been achieved. As Lieutenant John J. Pershing wrote,[16]

> White regiments, black regiments, regulars and Rough Riders, representing the young manhood of the North and South, fought shoulder to shoulder, unmindful of race or color, unmindful of whether commanded by an ex-Confederate or not, and mindful only of their common duty as Americans.

On the day following the battles of El Caney and San Juan
Heights, General Shafter was despondent. The Americans had been vic-
torious, but at very great cost. Moreover, because the surviving troops
were exhausted, Shafter did not want to launch an immediate attack
against the city. Instead, he wanted Admiral Sampson to move in
closer—enter the bay, in fact—engage Cervera, and then bombard the
enemy from the rear. Sampson refused to do so because he feared that
the entrance to the bay had been mined. He wanted Shafter to attack
the heights above the entrance to the bay so the navy would be free to
undertake a clearing operation, but Shafter refused, fearing heavy
losses. Neither the admiral nor the general was aware of the extreme
weakness of the Spanish garrison in and around the city. The defenders
numbered nearly 12,000, but they were desperately short of ammunition and supplies and many were sick.

Unable to agree upon an immediate action, Sampson and Shafter
decided to meet on the morning of July 3 to discuss their options.
Meanwhile, Shafter sent a message to the Spanish commander demanding that he surrender. As expected, General José Toral, who had
replaced General Linares because of the latter's illness, refused. The
meeting between Shafter and Sampson never took place that Sunday
morning because at 9:30 A.M. Admiral Cervera made his ill-fated dash
for the open sea and his squadron was completely destroyed. That battle changed everything. Shafter now decided to lay siege to the city
rather than launch an all-out assault. He offered Toral another chance
to surrender, which was again declined, and at about the same time he
received word that General Nelson Miles was on his way with reinforcements. These developments made victory absolutely certain. The
only question was how long it would take to persuade Toral to surrender. Shafter was concerned because he knew that the shadow of disease
hung over his men like the clouds of an ever-deepening storm.

During the next few days Shafter and representatives of the navy
led by Captain French Ensor Chadwick finally met and discussed possible scenarios for joint action, but none of these plans was ever carried
out. Shafter, still committed to the idea of a siege, devoted himself to
negotiating with the Spaniards, who he hoped would capitulate soon.
On July 8, much to Shafter's surprise, General Toral offered to surrender
the city to the Americans without resistance if, in return, his forces were
allowed to evacuate unmolested. Shafter was tempted to accept, but

McKinley ordered him to consider nothing short of unconditional surrender. Accordingly, Shafter notified Toral that unless he surrendered unconditionally, a naval bombardment would begin on the afternoon of July 10. There was no reply, so for three hours that day projectiles rained down upon the city. Later investigation revealed that damage was minimal. Nevertheless, on the July 11 Toral agreed to begin negotiations that would lead to surrender on July 17.

Meanwhile, two crucial events took place. The first was the arrival of General Miles with reinforcements and the second was the receipt of a message from Secretary of War Alger that authorized Shafter to offer an attractive proposal to Toral. If the Spanish commander would surrender the city, he and all his men would be returned to Spain at American expense rather than interned in a prison camp. Miles and Shafter communicated this proposal to Toral at a meeting held under a flag of truce on July 13. The Spaniard was obviously interested, but he informed the Americans that under Spanish law he could not give up as long as he possessed the means to resist. Upon hearing this the Americans agreed to extend the truce while Toral consulted his government.

The leading members of the Sagasta administration in Madrid were well aware that the war could not be won. Their main concern was how to end it without also losing all that remained of the Spanish empire. Some believed that an immediate surrender in Cuba might be the key. Perhaps then the Americans would forego an attack on Puerto Rico and agree to negotiate a settlement in the Philippines. The ministry was also concerned about the possibility of an American attack on Spain itself. In Havana Governor General Ramón Blanco y Erenas was doggedly determined to fight, but Sagasta and his colleagues overruled him. Permission to surrender was dispatched to Toral, who informed Shafter and Miles that he was ready to discuss terms.

The final negotiations were delayed for a short time because of a misunderstanding over the question of whether Spanish soldiers would be allowed to retain their weapons after the surrender. This issue was settled by a compromise agreement under which the arms were surrendered and later returned. Once this problem was overcome the discussions proceeded briskly. On the afternoon of July 16 representatives of the two parties met to conclude the final arrangements. Shafter sent generals Wheeler and Lawton as his representatives while Toral sent General Federico Escario and his aide. Both sides also had interpreters.

Admiral Sampson had wanted the navy to be represented, but Shafter ignored his request, and the ceremony was over before the government could order him to reconsider. The Cubans were also not represented.

In the written agreement the word surrender (*rendición*) does not appear because it would have humiliated the Spaniards. Instead, the agreement was termed a capitulation (*capitalación*) in order to spare Toral the inevitable criticism that would ensue even though he received permission to surrender. After the hostilities were formally concluded a group of Spanish soldiers even sent a message to the Americans praising their gallantry and congratulating them on their victory, while at the same time proclaiming that they had not been defeated.

Under the terms of the agreement Toral "surrendered" all his men and supplies in the area of Santiago and agreed to remove all mines from the harbor. The Americans agreed that all Spanish personnel would be sent home and their belongings returned. For the Spanish and for the Fifth Army Corps the war was over, but the Americans who remained had to confront the problem of surviving in Cuba until they could be evacuated. The problem was serious because, as General Shafter had feared, disease was beginning to take its toll.[17]

During the week following the capitulation, disease began to overtake the Fifth Army Corps. Although yellow fever was the greatest fear, there were actually more cases of malaria and dysentery, and the number of sick men ran quickly into the thousands. In letters to loved ones at home and to public officials the men demanded repatriation, and the newspapers soon picked up the story. Public opinion, which only a few weeks earlier had called for action, now demanded withdrawal. The men had done their job and there was no reason for them to suffer further. The government acted swiftly.

The process of evacuation began on August 7 when the first troops left for Montauk Point, Long Island. There the government was constructing a reception center known as Camp Wikoff, where the men would supposedly be nursed back to health before they returned home. By this time the Fifth Army Corps was a sorry lot, but eventually most recovered from their ordeal. Of the 20,000 men who passed through the camp by the end of September, only 257 died. On October 3 the Fifth Army Corps was formally disbanded and the men went home, with most arriving quietly. The enthusiasm that had characterized their departure was gone. Gaunt faces told of the horrors they had endured, and friends and relatives respected their desire for peace and quiet. The brief but savage battle for Cuba was indeed at an end, but the fighting in the Caribbean theater was not yet over.[18]

The War and Navy Departments had discussed the possibility of invading Puerto Rico early in 1898, but it did not become the object of serious consideration until April, when General John M. Schofield suggested that Puerto Rico and the Philippines should be the primary targets rather than Cuba. Because Schofield was a retired officer with an outstanding reputation, his proposal received immediate consideration. He argued that successful assaults against Puerto Rico and the Philippines might obviate the need to attack Cuba, which, after all, was the site of Spain's primary military strength in the Western Hemisphere. Schofield received support from Secretary of Navy Long, Captain Mahan, and General Miles.

Public attention, of course, centered on Cuba because of press coverage of the rebellion, and Puerto Rico received almost no attention until early May, when Admiral Sampson sailed out for a brief bombardment of San Juan. Later in the month, after Cervera arrived at Santiago, interest grew because the strategic importance of the island became clear. If it remained in Spanish hands it could serve indefinitely as a source of supply and respite for Spanish naval forces throughout the Caribbean. Nevertheless, McKinley and his closest advisers decided to send the main land force to Cuba because of the presence of Cervera's fleet. Only after Cervera had been destroyed and Cuba had fallen would an operation in Puerto Rico be permitted. At the same time, however, the administration decided to annex Puerto Rico at the conclusion of successful military operations there.

Late in June 1898, Miles received permission to prepare an expedition to Puerto Rico. At first, the plan was to launch a task force from U.S. ports, but after the fighting began in Cuba it was decided to send Miles's forces there in case they might be needed; they arrived between July 9 and July 11. Because of the Spanish surrender they saw no action, and Miles spent most of his time developing a final plan for the Puerto Rican campaign. Originally, he intended to land his forces at Farajado near the northeast corner of the island and then launch an assault against San Juan, the capital, where Spanish forces were concentrated. Miles wanted a strong naval escort on the voyage, and although Sampson was reluctant because there was no longer a Spanish naval threat, he was ordered to provide it. Miles left from Guantánamo on the afternoon of July 21 with a convoy of six ships, three of which carried troops and three of which made up the escort. At about the same time other forces departed from Charleston and Tampa, giving Miles a total force of 18,000 men. In Puerto Rico he would face Spanish defenders numbering about 9,000.

While en route Miles decided to land at Guánica rather than Farajado. Guánica was located near the southwest corner of the island, about as far away from San Juan as one could get. Exactly why Miles changed his plan in this way is not clear, but apparently he had concluded it would be best to avoid a frontal assault at San Juan. Many of Miles's colleagues were surprised and confused by this decision and unsuccessfully attempted to dissuade the general. On July 25 Miles landed at Guánica, where he encountered no opposition. During the next few days additional American forces went ashore at Ponce and Arroyo on the southern coast of the island to the east of the original site. From these locations Miles intended to send four columns north and east across the island. They would brush aside any opposition put up by Spanish forces and then concentrate for a combined assault on San Juan. These units were led by generals Theodore Schwan, George A. Garretson, Guy V. Henry, James H. Wilson, and John R. Brooks.

The Spanish defenders in Puerto Rico were under the command of Governor-General Manuel Macias y Casado. He chose to position his forces at four locations. Most were kept in the northeast near San Juan, but others were sent to the towns of Ponce, Mayaguez, and Caguas. By choosing this strategy Macias weakened his defensive capabilities considerably. Already outnumbered more than two to one, he probably should have concentrated all his strength at San Juan and forced the Americans to do battle there. As it was, the Spanish forces in the field were at a great disadvantage because they were so dispersed and because most of the native Puerto Ricans supported the Americans wherever they went. Macias, who soon realized that his situation was hopeless, relayed his assessment to Madrid, where Sagasta and his colleagues were already considering a request for an armistice.

What little fighting that occurred in Puerto Rico took place between August 5 and 12. The most serious engagement was fought near Coamo on August 7, where units under the command of General Wilson inflicted heavy casualties on the Spanish defenders. The Spanish forces lost 40 killed and wounded. The next day Schwan's forces fought a brief engagement near Mayaguez, where the Spanish suffered 50 casualties and the Americans 17. There were no further hostilities because Spanish and American negotiators meeting in Washington signed an armistice at about 4:30 in the afternoon on August 12.

General Miles's invasion of Puerto Rico was a great success. There were only 43 casualties: seven killed and 36 wounded, and there were no significant medical problems. The landings had gone much more smoothly than those in Cuba, and the Puerto Rican people, for the most part, welcomed the Americans as liberators. On the other hand, there was one striking similarity to the Cuban campaign: once the fighting ended there was immediate and intense pressure placed on Washington to "bring the boys home." As a result the volunteers were evacuated very quickly and replaced with regulars, who temporarily acted as an army of occupation. The armistice agreement had specified that Spanish forces would leave as soon as possible, and within sixty days all of them were gone.[19]

Notes

1. Trask, *The War with Spain in 1898,* pp. 145–58.
2. ———., pp. 158–62.
3. ———., pp. 167–77.
4. For a thorough description of conditions at Tampa see *ibid.,* pp. 178–93.
5. Millis, *The Martial Spirit,* pp. 244–48.
6. ———., pp. 247–48.
7. O'Toole, *The Spanish War,* p. 244.
8. Trask, *The War with Spain in 1898,* p. 212.
9. Frank Freidel, *The Splendid Little War* (Boston: Little, Brown and Company, 1958), p. 85.
10. Trask, *The War with Spain in 1898,* pp. 203–206.
11. ———., p. 221.
12. Freidel, *The Splendid Little War,* pp. 108–9.
13. ———., pp. 119–42.
14. ———., p. 140.
15. Trask, *The War with Spain in 1898,* pp. 238–56.
16. Freidel, *The Splendid Little War,* p. 173.
17. O'Toole, *The Spanish War,* pp. 340–50.
18. Trask, *The War with Spain in 1898,* pp. 324–35.
19. ———., pp. 336–68.

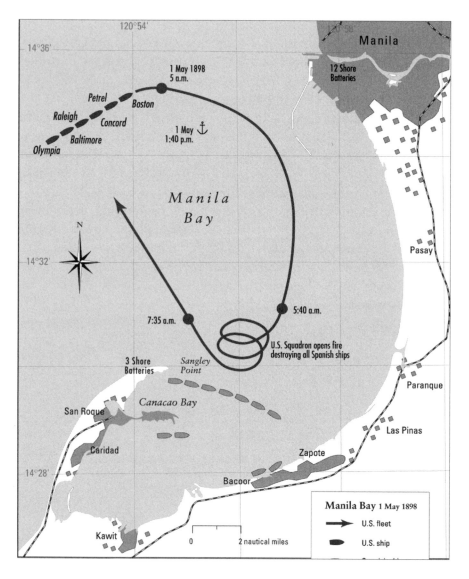

The Battle of Manila Bay

CHAPTER 4

NAVAL ACTION: THE BATTLES OF MANILA BAY AND SANTIAGO DE CUBA

Having been advised to prepare an attack on the Spanish fleet at Manila in case of war, Commodore George Dewey was ready when his orders arrived on April 25, 1898: "War has commenced between the United States and Spain. Proceed at once, particularly against Spanish fleet. You must capture vessels or destroy. Use utmost endeavor."[1]

Dewey left Hong Kong on April 27 in command of a nine-ship squadron that included four protected cruisers: *Olympia*, his flagship; *Baltimore*; *Raleigh*; and *Boston*; the unprotected cruiser *Concord*; the gunboat *Petrel*; the revenue cutter *McCulloch*; the supply ship *Zafiro*; and the collier *Naushan*. Dewey felt confident, but his optimism was not shared by everyone, including the British friends he had just left behind. Later, he wrote, "In the Hong Kong Club it was not possible to get bets even at heavy odds, that our expedition would be a success . . . I was told, after our officers had been entertained at dinner by a British regiment, that the universal remark among our hosts was . . . 'A fine set of fellows but unhappily we shall never see them again.'"[2]

In fact Dewey and his men were in no danger of defeat provided the commodore conducted his operation skillfully. Those who should have been truly worried were the officers and men who manned the decrepit little fleet under the command of Admiral Patricio Montojo at Manila. Montojo had at his disposal two unprotected cruisers, *Reina Cristina* and *Castilla*, and five gunboats, *Don Juan de Austria, Don Antonio de Ulloa, Isla de Cuba, Marqués del Duero*, and *Isla de Luza*. A comparison between this squadron and Dewey's revealed an overwhelming advantage in favor of the Americans. The six fighting vessels in the American fleet outweighed the Spanish ships by more than 7,000 tons; all of them were faster and more modern; and, most important of all, there was a great difference in armaments. Dewey's cruisers carried eight-inch guns that were more powerful and had a greater range than anything the Spanish commander had at his disposal. Finally, the American sailors were better trained and the American officers were more competent than their adversaries.

Aware of his weakness, Admiral Montojo knew he faced almost certain defeat, if not annihilation, but nevertheless devoted considerable thought to planning his defense. His original intent was to confront the Americans in Subig Bay some 35 miles from Manila. He took his ships there on April 25, but when he arrived he discovered that the new shore batteries he expected to find were not ready, so he returned to Manila Bay. By April 28, Montojo knew that Dewey was on his way and had to consider his remaining options, none of which was particularly attractive. He could have fled Manila Bay, forcing Dewey to chase him, but this plan was vigorously opposed by Governor General Basilio Augustín, who unrealistically seemed to believe that somehow Montojo could withstand an American onslaught. Montojo could have left the harbor and fought in the open sea, but he knew such a move would simply invite disaster, so he abandoned that idea. His other options were to fight at the mouth of the harbor near the island of Corregidor, under the protection of the shore batteries at Manila, or to anchor in the shallow water off nearby Cavite and force the Americans to attack him there. Montojo rejected the first of these options because the water near Corregidor was very deep and there would be greater loss of life, and the second because he feared the American gunners might hit the city of Manila, killing many civilians. After giving these ideas much consideration and consulting with his captains, Montojo decided to force an action off Cavite.

Dewey arrived at Subig Bay on April 30, discovered that Montojo was not there, and moved on. At midnight he entered Manila Bay, and soon thereafter he called his captains together to issue their orders. Joseph L. Stickney of the *New York Herald*, who was with Dewey on the *Olympia*, later wrote, "The war council was of short duration. Commodore Dewey had decided on his plans before it met, and he took little time in giving each captain his duties for the night and the next day."[3]

As Dewey's ships entered Manila Bay under cover of darkness they passed shore batteries mounted on the island of Corregidor. They also faced the possible danger of mines, but there was no opposition and Dewey was amazed when he was later told that many of the enemy batteries were not even manned that dark April night. The Americans sailed slowly across the bay at a speed of eight knots because the commodore did not want to reach his objective before daybreak. The battle formation was led by *Olympia*, followed at spaces of 200 to 400 yards by *Baltimore, Petrel, Raleigh, Concord*, and *Boston*. At 5:40 A.M., when *Olympia* was about 5,000 yards away from the enemy, Dewey uttered the words that were to make him world famous—"You may fire when ready, Gridley"[4]—and *Olympia's* eight-inch guns began the attack.

In all, the American ships made five sorties past the Spaniards, who were riding at anchor, between 5:40 A.M. and 12:30 P.M. on May 1. Early in the action Admiral Montojo ordered his flagship, *Reina Cristina*, to leave its position and attack *Olympia*, but the Spanish vessel, raked by fire from all the American ships, was badly damaged and forced to break off the attack. Before the battle was over *Reina Cristina* was sunk, along with *Castilla* and *Don Antonio de Ulloa*. All the other Spanish ships were badly damaged, and Spanish casualties were high. Montojo lost not only all his ships, but also 161 killed and 210 wounded. The Americans, on the other hand, were practically unscathed. No one was killed, nine men were wounded, and there was little damage to the American ships, so inaccurate had been the Spanish fire. But in the aftermath of the battle, the Americans realized that their gunnery had been none too accurate either. Lieutenant Bradley A. Fiske, who was on *Petrel*, wrote later, "I think everybody was disappointed at the great number of shots lost. Our practice was evidently much better than that of the Spaniards, but it did not seem to me that it was all that good.'"[5] This poor shooting was cause for serious concern.

Dewey's victory made American control of the Philippines a possibility, but he could proceed no further without additional forces. Therefore, he requested ground troops, which were immediately dispatched.

Dewey understood clearly what he had done. He wrote later, "From the moment that the captain-general accepted my terms the city was virtually surrounded and I was in control of the situation subject to my government's orders for its future."[6]

The victory also made Dewey an instant national hero. He was promoted to the rank of admiral and for a short time a "Dewey for president" surge swept the nation. This euphoria did not last long, but it generated even greater public support for the war than already existed. As for poor Admiral Montojo, he was court-martialed upon his return to Spain for dereliction of duty. Of course, no one had realistically expected him to win, but it was customary in Spain to punish military commanders who lost. Montojo's defense rested on claims that he was hopelessly outgunned by the American ships, that he had received inadequate reinforcements from the home government, and that selecting any other option for battle would have led to even more devastation. Also, his government had to admit that he fought bravely and was wounded in action. He was convicted, but his punishment was merely to be discharged from the military.

Meanwhile, the focus shifted to the Caribbean Sea. In that theater naval action developed in two phases: the blockade of Cuba and the naval battle of Santiago de Cuba, where the two American commanders were Admiral William T. Sampson and Commodore Winfield Scott Schley. Admiral Pascual Cervera y Topete led the Spanish forces. On April 26, 1898, President McKinley proclaimed a blockade of Cuba to prevent supplies and reinforcements from reaching Spanish forces stationed there. A group designated as the North Atlantic Squadron under the command of Sampson was dispatched from Key West to impose the blockade while a second battle group known as the Flying Squadron, under the command of Commodore Schley, continued to operate off the coast of Virginia to protect against a possible attack by a Spanish fleet.

On April 29, three days after McKinley proclaimed the blockade, Admiral Cervera left the Cape Verde Islands bound for San Juan, Puerto Rico, thought by the Spanish Ministry of Marine to be the most likely target of an American attack at the beginning of the war. His force was pathetically weak when compared to the forces at the disposal of Sampson and Schley. It consisted of four armored cruisers and three destroy-ers, all of which were obsolete. Cervera knew from the beginning of his mission that if he ever encountered the Americans he would be destroyed.

As soon as the U.S. navy learned of Cervera's departure they pre-pared to intercept him. Sampson, whose squadron was already cruising off northern Cuba, departed for Puerto Rico, hoping to engage the Spanish fleet there. When he did so he was cautioned by Secretary of the Navy Long to be careful lest Cervera slip by him and go on to Cuba. Meanwhile, Cervera detoured to the French island of Martinique, hop-ing to find supplies and coal. When he arrived there he discovered that Cuba was blockaded, Sampson was at San Juan, and there was no coal. He went on to the Dutch island of Curacáo in further search of coal, deciding to avoid Puerto Rico and a possible encounter with Sampson. Once again he found no coal and was told by the Dutch authorities that he could not stay. He then opted to make for the harbor at Santiago on the southern coast of Cuba. There he would not be safe, but at least he could buy some time.

On May 12 , while Cervera was at Martinique, Sampson arrived at Puerto Rico. Finding that the Spanish fleet was not there, he fired a few shots at the Spanish fortifications in the harbor at San Juan and then considered his next move. Later the same day he sailed for Haiti, found no Spanish forces, and moved on toward his home base at Key West, arriving on May 18. Unknown to Sampson, Schley had been ordered to Key West as well, and he arrived the same day.

While at Key West the two American officers received orders for their next move. The plan was for Schley to take the Flying Squadron to the waters south of Cuba and blockade the port of Cienfuegos. This move was important because the only railroad running south from Havana terminated at Cienfuegos. But while Schley was en route it became clear that Cervera had gone to Santiago. Thus Sampson ordered Schley to go there at once and bottle up Cervera in the harbor. Schley received the order on May 24 but did not take up a station off Santiago until May 29. His behavior during that five-day period was very erratic and caused much confusion among his subordinate officers and anxiety for Sampson and Secretary Long. What had happened?

When Schley received his orders to move from Cienfuegos to Santiago he was uncertain of Cervera's exact location. Because he believed that the Spanish squadron might still be in the harbor at Cienfuegos, he hesitated to leave. On the evening of May 24, two days before he finally concluded that Cervera was gone, he sailed east toward Santiago. He arrived two days later but decided almost at once to go on to Key West to obtain coal. His subordinates in command of the other vessels in his squadron were now becoming very confused. Schley did not take them into his confidence and they were unsure of his plans. Moreover, when Sampson and Long learned what he was doing, they sent urgent messages advising him to stay at Santiago. It was vital, they pointed out, to be certain of Cervera's whereabouts. As a result, Schley turned his squadron around, returned to Santiago, and established a blockade on May 29. Meanwhile, Sampson left Key West and joined Schley off Santiago on June 1. The force he commanded now included the battleship *Oregon,* which had just arrived after a lengthy voyage around Cape Horn; the armored cruiser *New York;* and two smaller vessels. Schley's command included the battleships *Massachusetts, Iowa,* and *Texas;* the armored cruiser *Brooklyn,* Schley's flagship; three less powerful cruisers, *New Orleans, Marblehead,* and *Howard;* and two smaller vessels. This combined force was so overwhelming compared to Cervera's seven-vessel squadron that no meaningful comparison could be made.

While Schley was meandering around along the southern coast of Cuba between May 23 and May 29, Cervera had numerous opportunities to escape, but he and his commanders rejected them all for various reasons, the most important of which was very simple: they lacked the necessary supplies for a return trip to Spain, and they knew that to be caught in the open sea by the Americans meant certain disaster. Therefore, Cervera decided to stay at Santiago as long as possible and assist with the defense of the city against an expected attack by the Americans from the landward side.

The actual blockade of the harbor at Santiago lasted from May 29 until July 3, 1898. It was planned and executed under the orders of Admiral Sampson and was very successful. Sampson divided his forces into two groups: Schley commanded a division made up of *Brooklyn; Massachusetts; Texas; Marblehead; Gloucester;* and a small armed yacht, *Vixen.* Sampson himself commanded a group consisting of *New York;*

Iowa; Oregon; and two smaller ships, *Mayflower* and *Porter.* He positioned all these ships in an arc eight miles from end to end around the entrance to the harbor at a distance of six miles. Each night certain vessels moved closer and trained their searchlights on the harbor entrance, making it virtually impossible for Cervera to come out undetected. Sampson also decided to sink a derelict vessel in the mouth of the harbor to make an exit even more difficult. This risky operation was carried out by a small group of volunteers led by Lieutenant Richmond P. Hobson. Unfortunately, their bravery was wasted because the hulk went down at a place where it did not completely block the harbor entrance. Hobson and his men were captured but later exchanged. Meanwhile, the Americans periodically bombarded Spanish coastal positions but did relatively little damage and certainly did not cause the enemy to consider surrender.

The U.S. army ground forces landed at Daiquirí on June 22, 1898, and began their drive toward the city of Santiago. They moved inexorably westward and by July 1 commanded the heights overlooking the city. Their success placed the defenders within the city as well as Admiral Cervera and his squadron in grave danger. Both would soon have to decide whether to fight or surrender, and neither option was very attractive. Conflict meant certain destruction and surrender meant dishonor, an unacceptable outcome.

Unfortunately for Admiral Cervera and his men, they were now under the command of Governor General Ramón Blanco y Erenas, who had decided that they must engage the enemy. Cervera used all his persuasive powers to dissuade the governor but had no success. Finally, he was forced to comply, but in his final statement he left no doubt as to his opinion: "I state most emphatically that I shall never be the one to decree the horrible and useless hecatomb which will be the only possible result of the Sortie, from here by main force, for I should consider myself responsible before God and history, for the lives sacrificed on the altar of vanity and not in true defense of the country."[7]

Cervera issued his orders on the evening of July 2. The plan was to leave the harbor the following morning, a Sunday, at 9:00 A.M. He hoped a departure at this time might catch the Americans unprepared because he knew they would be in the midst of religious services and inspection. His ships would have to leave the narrow entrance in single file one at a time and would be led by *Infanta María Teresa* followed by *Vizcaya, Cristóbal Colón,* and *Almirante Oquendo.* The two small destroyers *Furor* and *Plutón* would be in the rear. The larger ships would engage the enemy and the speedy destroyers would attempt to escape. It was perfectly clear to Cervera, his officers, and most of his men that this plan offered almost no hope of success, but they had decided there were no other options.

The Americans first caught sight of *Infanta María Teresa* at 9:35 A.M. Captain Robley D. Evans, in command of the battleship *Iowa*, recorded his reaction: "I had just finished having breakfast, and was sitting smoking at my cabin table, in conversation with my son, a naval cadet, . . . (when) . . . the general alarm for action rang all over the ship . . . We both started as fast as we could go to the bridge . . . at this moment the Spanish cruiser *Infanta María Teresa* was in plain view . . . her magnificent battle flag showing clear . . . as I reached the bridge."[8]

At that very moment Captain Victor Concas, in command of Cervera's flagship, asked permission to open fire, and the battle was joined. Ironically, Admiral Sampson, the American commander, was not in a position to participate because earlier that morning he had taken his flagship *New York* eastward along the coast, planning to go ashore for a conference with General Shafter. When he heard the firing begin he reversed course, but before he could close to effective range, the battle was over. His maneuvers left Commodore Schley in command, and because the two were not on friendly terms, what happened next precipitated a dispute between them that would drag on for years after the war.

As the Spanish vessels began leaving from the harbor seven American warships awaited them. These included, in addition to *Iowa*, the battleships *Indiana, Oregon,* and *Texas;* the armored cruiser *Brooklyn*, Schley's flagship; and two converted yachts, *Gloucester* and *Vixen.* All of Cervera's ships turned to starboard (right) as they emerged and fled down the coast in a westerly direction. This maneuver required the Americans to execute a turn to port (left) to pursue them, but for some inexplicable reason Schley ordered *Brooklyn* to turn right, placing his ship between Cervera and the battleships *Texas* and *Iowa* and nearly causing a collision. When later he was asked to explain his unlikely maneuver, Schley blithely declared that it placed him on a course parallel to the enemy and determined the outcome of the battle. Because the battle resulted in an overwhelming American victory Schley was only mildly rebuked. If the outcome had been different, his overall performance during the blockade and the battle might well have led to a court-martial.

As Schley executed his peculiar maneuver *Infanta María Teresa* remained under fire from the entire American squadron. Soon disabled, Cervera's flagship ran aground at 10:35 A.M., just one hour after coming out of the harbor. Meanwhile, two additional Spanish ships appeared and fled west. These were *Vizcaya* and *Cristóbal Colón*. At first they received little fire, but the fourth Spanish warship to emerge, *Almirante Oquendo,* was disabled almost at once and ran aground at 10:40 A.M. Of the Spanish destroyers, *Plutón* was grounded at 10:45 A.M. and *Furor* sank in deep water shortly thereafter. By 11:00 A.M. *Vizcaya* and *Cristóbal Colón* were still in flight. *Vizcaya* suffered a withering barrage and ran aground at 11:15 A.M. Captain Evans of *Iowa* described the carnage:[9]

> The ship had grounded about four hundred yards from the beach, and between her and the shore was a sand pit on which many had taken refuge . . . The Cuban insurgents had opened fire on them from the shore, and with a glass I could plainly see the bullets sniping the water among them. The sharks, made ravenous by the blood of the wounded, were attacking them from the outside. Many of the wounded still remained on deck . . . and were likely to be burned to death by the rapidly heating ship . . .

Of the 2,227 Spanish sailors and officers who participated in this engagement, 323 were killed and 151 wounded. Most of the survivors, approximately 1,720, were rescued by the Americans, but a few went ashore in hostile territory. Among those rescued was Admiral Cervera, who seemed happy that the ordeal was over. Lieutenant Harry P. Huse of *Gloucester* remembered: "Far from being depressed, the Admiral was in high spirits. He had done his duty to the utmost limits, and was relieved of the terrible burden of responsibility that had weighed upon him since leaving the Cape Verde Islands."[10]

The victory, which resulted from the overwhelming superiority of American firepower and the careful planning of Admiral Sampson, was the most significant battle of the war but was marred by controversy. When Commodore Schley signaled Sampson that his forces had triumphed, Sampson's reply was simply, "Report your casualties." Schley regarded this as an affront and never forgave it. On the other hand, one of Sampson's subordinate officers sent a message to McKinley in the admiral's name that was not well received. "The fleet under my command offers the nation on a Fourth of July present the whole of Cervera's fleet."[11] To many this boastful statement seemed to ignore the fact that Sampson had not actually participated in the battle, and his reputation among his colleagues and the public never fully recovered. Conversely, Schley, who had bungled repeatedly since the last week of May, received most of the plaudits at home.

The victories of American naval forces in the battles of Manila Bay and Santiago had far-reaching military and geopolitical consequences. On the military side was the matter of gunnery. Even though the Spanish squadrons were easily destroyed in both battles, the percentage of hits scored by American gunners (relative to total shots fired) was very low. This failure led to immediate changes in the training and preparation of naval gunners. More important were the geopolitical consequences. The elimination of the Spanish naval threat made possible the conquest of any Spanish territory the Americans might want and changed the nature of the war from a struggle to free the oppressed Cubans from Spanish domination to one of territorial expansion. This was an outcome not clearly envisioned when the United States declared war on Spain in April.[12]

Notes

1. Freidel, *The Splendid Little War,* p. 15.
2. ———., p.14.
3. ———., p. 17.
4. O'Toole, *The Spanish War,* p. 185.
5. Trask, *The War with Spain in 1898,* p. 104.
6. ———., p. 105.
7. ———., p. 258.
8. Freidel, *The Splendid Little War,* p. 193.
9. ———., p. 226.

10. ———., p. 228.

11. Trask, *The War with Spain in 1898*, p. 266.

12. The material in this chapter is drawn from the following sources: Frank Freidel, *The Splendid Little War*, pp. 193–232; David Trask, *The War with Spain in 1898*, pp. 257–269; and D. J. A. O'Toole, *The Spanish War*, pp. 323–39.

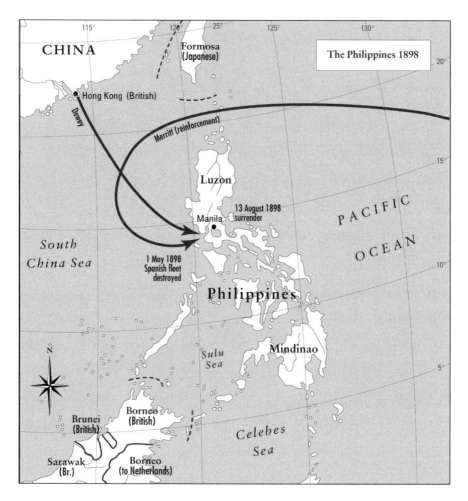

The Approach of U.S. Forces to the Philippines

CHAPTER 5

CAMPAIGNING IN THE PHILIPPINES

After the Battle of Manila Bay on May 1, 1898, Commodore Dewey informed the government that he could easily hold his position but that reinforcements would be required to take the city of Manila. "We had the city under our guns," he wrote. " . . . But naval power can reach no further ashore. For tenure of the land you must have the man with a rifle."[1] He then proceeded to force the surrender of the Spanish batteries at Corregidor; cut the communications cable between Manila and Hong Kong; and move his squadron to Cavite, which was out of range of the Spanish guns at Manila.

The Spanish defenders at Manila were under the command of Governor General Basilio Augustín, who knew he faced a difficult task. He also knew that his position was hopeless unless he received help from Spain. Prime Minister Sagasta and his advisers understood the problem and late in May dispatched a naval squadron under Admiral Manuel de la Camará. This squadron went as far as the Suez Canal and then turned back when the Spanish government realized that without Camará's ships the home waters could not be defended against a possible American attack. When Augustín learned of Camará's return to Spain, he gave up all hope. He wrote, "I insist on the doleful consequences at [the] end of this situation because of scarce defense elements becoming exhausted and not receiving assistance."[2]

Meanwhile, as Dewey awaited his reinforcements, naval units from a number of countries entered Manila Bay to observe conditions and report to their governments. By the end of June five German ships, three British ships, and two additional vessels from France and Japan were in the harbor. The German squadron was the most worrisome because it was far superior to Dewey's force, and the commodore had no idea of the intentions of the German commander, Vice-Admiral Otto von Diederichs. In actuality, Diederichs had been ordered to the Philippines to gather information about conditions there and assist his government in forming a future Far East policy. Without doubt the German government wanted to be the most powerful neutral country on the scene should the Americans decide not to annex the Philippines, but Diederichs had no orders to interfere with American operations.

Dewey understandably was nervous about the presence of such a powerful German force. He became further agitated when he received word that the Germans had contacted the Filipinos for some reason— he never learned why—and this led to heated exchanges between representatives of the two commanders, who met to try to calm the situation. Dewey later recalled,[3]

> I made the most of the occasion by using him as a third person to state candidly and firmly my attitude in a verbal message which he conveyed to his superiors so successfully that . . . Diederichs was able to understand my point of view. There was no further interference with the blockade or breach of the etiquette which had been established by the common consent of the other foreign commanders. Thus, as I explained to the President, after the war was over, a difference of opinion about international law had been adjusted amicably, without adding to the sum of his worries.

Luckily, nothing stronger than words was exchanged, and what could have been a real crisis fizzled. During the remainder of the conflict the Germans did nothing to impede American activities.

Meanwhile, McKinley and his advisers quickly developed a plan to support Dewey. Before May 1 the president had given no thought to the possibility of military operations in the Philippines, but now all that had changed. On May 12, he chose General Wesley Merritt to lead a Philippine expedition numbering about 20,000 men, of whom nearly half were volunteers. They left from San Francisco in several contingents, beginning on May 25, for the monthlong voyage to Manila. This was the first time in American history that such a long-range invasion of enemy territory had been attempted, and it went amazingly well. At San Francisco there were no bottlenecks or supply problems such as those that befuddled General Shafter at Tampa. The only real problem in the voyage was seasickness. A signal corps sergeant described the scene as Merritt's forces departed on June 29:[4]

> What a magnificent send-off San Francisco gave us as we sailed out of the harbor. . . . The numberless streamers, the guns, flags flying everywhere, handkerchiefs waving. . . . Then the boys in the *Indiana* realized what the parting really meant, but we did not dwell long on that, for as we passed [through the Golden Gate] a strong wind was blowing which steadily increased. After crossing the bar the sea was very rough, and I think nine hundred and ninety nine of the thousand men aboard were sea-sick.

As Merritt and his men slowly steamed across the Pacific, Congress took what proved to be an important step: it annexed the Hawaiian Islands. The U.S. presence in Hawaii dated back more than 50 years and was based largely on economic interests represented by sugar and fruit production, and strategic considerations represented by Pearl Harbor. In 1875 a treaty between the United States and the Kingdom of Hawaii had made the islands a virtual American protectorate, and American interests there grew rapidly. A coup in 1892 overthrew the monarchy, and the leaders—mostly American businessmen—sought annexation. This effort was supported by President Benjamin Harrison, but he was defeated for reelection in 1892, and his successor, Grover Cleveland, opposed territorial expansion. The annexation movement then collapsed and the coup leaders were forced to create the Republic of Hawaii, which lasted from 1893 to 1898. The outbreak of war with Spain and the now obvious strategic interests of the United States in the Pacific resurrected interest and Congress responded with a joint resolution. The House passed it on June 15, the Senate on July 6, and President McKinley signed it on July 7. On doing so he remarked, "We need Hawaii just as much and a good deal more than we did California. It is manifest destiny."[5]

The United States took control of another island possession as a result of the Philippine campaign. On June 20 the cruiser *Charleston*, flagship of the Pacific squadron heading for Manila, arrived off Agaña, capital of the tiny island of Guam, a Spanish possession in the Marianas. Captain Henry Glass took his ship into the harbor of San Luis d'Apra and lobbed a few shells at an unoccupied fort. The Spanish officials on shore did not know they were at war and thought the American shots represented some kind of salute. When they came aboard the *Charleston* to welcome their visitors, Glass informed them of their situation, and they promptly surrendered. Two days later Glass resumed his voyage to the Philippines.

The first American contingent, a group consisting of slightly more than 3,000 men commanded by General Thomas M. Anderson, arrived on June 30. Others arrived periodically, and by July 31 the American force on the ground numbered approximately 11,000. When Merritt arrived with his group on July 25, he took command of operations. He soon had to make two major decisions: the first was to devise quickly an overall plan of operations, and the second was to decide how, if at all, to utilize the Filipino insurgents under the command of Emilio Aguinaldo. These decisions came quickly: Merritt would launch a ground attack with naval support, and he would not involve the insurgents if at all possible. This decision was undoubtedly correct—given American policy—but it was later to lead to unspeakable carnage because of the intense desire of many Filipinos for independence.

There had been a long history of unrest among the Filipinos before the late 1890s. One nationalist organization that played a major role during the decade was the *Katipunan*, founded in 1892. *Katipunan* is a word from the Tagalog language, the indigenous language of the people, meaning "society of the sons of the people." One of its leaders was Andrés Bonifacio, a young man from the working class who favored armed rebellion. He became president of the society on January 1, 1896, and soon began planning a violent uprising. Unfortunately for him, the authorities uncovered his plan, and he was forced to flee into the backcountry even though his followers began military operations. Among them was Emilio Aguinaldo y Famy, who came from an upperclass, land-owning family.

The governor general of the Philippines in 1896 was Ramón Blanco y Erenas, who would later be sent to Cuba. During the summer and fall of that year Blanco attempted without success to stamp out the rebellion. In early November Aguinaldo commanded an insurgent force that inflicted heavy casualties on the Spaniards. This victory led to his rise to power. At the same time the Spanish government replaced Blanco with General Camilo de Polavieja, a much more aggressive individual, who set out to crush the rebellion. By the spring of 1897 his efforts had so weakened the insurgent forces that they could no longer carry out conventional military operations.

During this stressful period an internal power struggle pitting Aguinaldo against Bonifacio resulted in the court-martial and execution of the latter. Aguinaldo then led his forces into the mountains and prepared to wage guerrilla warfare. Meanwhile, Fernando Primo de Rivera, who had replaced Polavieja as governor general, agreed to consider a negotiated settlement. Between August and December of 1897 intermediaries scurried back and forth between Manila and Aguinaldo's stronghold at Biyak-na-Bató. Aguinaldo demanded several reforms, including autonomy, the redistribution of church land, and civil rights, while Primo de Rivera simply wanted an end to hostilities. The home government agreed to a settlement because they thought they had much bigger problems in Cuba.

Aguinaldo and Primo de Rivera concluded an agreement known as the Pact of Biyak-na-Bató in December 1897. Under this agreement Aguinaldo agreed to go into exile in Hong Kong in exchange for a payment of 800,000 Mexican pesos and a vague promise from the Spanish to carry out some reforms. In making these agreements each party fully intended to deceive the other. Aguinaldo intended to use the money to plan and finance further revolutionary activities while Primo de Rivera did not intend to institute reforms. He did hand over 400,000 pesos to Aguinaldo and 200,000 to other Filipino leaders, but he never delivered the final installment of 200,000 pesos to anybody. A brief period of calm followed the Pact of Biyak-na-Bató, but by March 1898 the rebels were back in action. Aguinaldo, still in Hong Kong, made his first contact with the Americans at this time. What happened thereafter has continued to be a subject of great controversy.

Aguinaldo later claimed that Colonel Leonard Wood, one of Dewey's officers, tried to induce him to return to the Philippines and lead a new revolt with American aid. There is no evidence to support this claim, but in any event, Aguinaldo left Hong Kong in April bound not for home but for Europe. En route he stopped at Singapore, where he met the U.S. consul general, E. Spencer Pratt, who urged him to return to Hong Kong and discuss matters with Commodore Dewey. Aguinaldo agreed to go back if Dewey invited him, and Pratt urged Dewey to do so. Dewey agreed, and Aguinaldo departed on April 27. He later claimed that he returned to Hong Kong with a clear understanding that the United States was now committed to Filipino independence. E. Spencer Pratt had no authority to make any such guarantee and always claimed that he had not done so. There is no persuasive evidence upon which to base a conclusion either way.

Dewey left for Manila before Aguinaldo arrived at Hong Kong, but later, via an American vessel carrying dispatches back and forth, authorized the Filipino leader to continue his journey. Aguinaldo landed at Cavite on May 19, and from that day on the American war with Spain and the Philippine revolution were irrevocably intertwined. Aguinaldo never deviated from his claim that the Americans had promised to fight for Philippine independence.

Late in May Dewey and Aguinaldo concluded a vague agreement of cooperation, and shortly thereafter Aguinaldo proclaimed himself dictator of an interim government that would deliver power to a democratically elected government once the Spaniards were driven out. In the same proclamation he referred to the Americans as friends who had come to offer aid and who believed the Filipinos to be capable of governing themselves. His army then began operations. They fought several successful engagements in the vicinity of Manila and then laid siege to the city. Dewey gave them encouragement, but little more. He believed they lacked the strength to take Manila and that the issue would not be finally decided until the arrival of the American reinforcements. He wrote to Secretary Long, "Have acted according to the spirit of the Department's instructions from the beginning, and I have entered into no alliance with the insurgents or any faction."[6]

When General Anderson arrived on June 30, he conferred with Aguinaldo and found him to be outwardly cooperative but at the same time not entirely forthcoming. Anderson soon began to suspect that Aguinaldo desperately wanted to take Manila without American help. Merritt, who arrived on July 25, agreed, and he began at once to develop his plan to take the city without including Aguinaldo. These strange circumstances were to lead to a bizarre end to the campaign and eventually to a conflict between the Filipinos and the Americans that would be far bloodier and more brutal than the conflict with Spain.

Inside Manila morale had reached a very low point. With the arrival of Merritt and receipt of the news that Camará was not coming, Augustín, who with his men had lost all hope, requested permission from Madrid to negotiate a truce. As a result he was replaced by Don Fermín Jáudenes y Alvarez. The government had lost confidence in Augustín and, in any case, did not want to give up in the Philippines before the conclusion of a peace protocol in Washington.

The American commanders sent two notes to Jáudenes—one on August 6 and another on August 9—demanding surrender. At some time between those two dates the governor general devised a plan to end the hopeless struggle without subjecting himself to later recriminations: he would surrender if the Americans would participate in a sham battle to preserve Spanish honor and agree to keep the Filipinos out of the city. The Americans accepted these terms, although they were not entirely certain that Jáudenes would keep his word.

The plan was for Dewey to bombard an unmanned fort just south of the city for a short time and then ask for surrender. Meanwhile, two columns of infantry led by generals Arthur MacArthur and Francis V. Greene would approach Manila. The Filipinos would be told to stand aside. The charade began early on the morning of August 13. Dewey bombarded the fort for one hour with no return fire, and a little later Greene and MacArthur began their advance. They were fired upon by Spanish defenders and sustained a few casualties, but by early afternoon they entered the city. The defenders formally surrendered at about 2:30 P.M. Aguinaldo's men, who did not participate in these activities, clearly were not happy and maintained their position throughout.

The formal terms of surrender were signed by Merritt and Jáudenes on August 14. Neither man was aware that their battle actually had taken place after the signing of a peace protocol in Washington on August 12. This situation raised important questions of international law because if the victory in the Philippines occurred after the signing of the protocol, then technically the islands had not been conquered. When word of the protocol finally arrived on August 16, Jáudenes offered a feeble protest to some of the terms of their surrender, but nothing more. The issue, however, would be thoroughly debated in the peace conference that began in Paris on October 1.[7]

Notes

1. Trask, *The War with Spain in 1898,* p. 370.
2. ———., p. 373.

3. O'Toole, *The Spanish War,* p. 366.

4. Freidel, *The Splendid Little War,* p. 284.

5. Leech, *In the Days of McKinley,* p. 212.

6. Trask, *The War with Spain in 1898,* p. 405.

7. The material in this chapter is based upon David Trask, *The War with Spain in 1898,* pp. 369–422; and Frank Freidel, *The Splendid Little War,* pp. 279–94.

CHAPTER 6

MAKING PEACE

Once the U.S. navy had gained superiority in the Caribbean and the Western Pacific, it was almost certain that McKinley, who wanted a short war, would achieve his objective. The first peace terms that he hoped to impose on Spain were offered on June 3, 1898. Spain was to evacuate Cuba, cede Puerto Rico to the United States, give the United States the use of port facilities in the Philippines, and cede an island in the Marianas. Eventually, it would be decided that the United States would take the entire Philippine archipelago—a major change—but otherwise the terms remained the same until the completion of peace negotiations in Paris later in the year.

For some weeks there was no reaction to the American proposals from Madrid, but on July 18 Sagasta instructed his ambassador in Paris, Francisco Jean y Castillo, to contact the French ambassador in Washington, Jules Cambon, and request that he inform the Americans that Spain was willing to negotiate. The French were handling matters for Spain as a courtesy because during the war there were, of course, no diplomatic relations between the United States and Spain. In addition, on July 26, McKinley received a letter from the Queen Regent herself asking for terms. McKinley then met with his cabinet to discuss exactly what should be done. It was in these discussions that the emotional arguments concerning the question of whether the United States should seize the Philippines emerged. The administration as well as public opinion was divided on the issue, and McKinley discovered that it would not be easy to make a satisfactory decision.

Generally, those who favored annexation of the Philippines argued that the United States had no alternative. The islands could not be returned to Spain; that would be dishonorable, and the Dutch, Russians, Germans, and French must not be allowed to gain a foothold there. Hence, the only viable options were to annex the islands outright, or hold them in trust until the native inhabitants could demonstrate their ability to rule themselves. Those who opposed holding on to the Philippines argued that the spirit of the Teller amendment should apply to all the territories where the United States fought to overpower the Spaniards. Otherwise, the Americans would have to admit that the conflict with Spain was nothing more than a war of naked aggression and conquest despite all the flowery pronouncements to the contrary.

McKinley presented the American terms to Cambon on July 30—the same as those of June 3—and the Frenchman responded with arguments reflecting Spanish interests. The president's reaction clearly indicated his resolve. He told Cambon that the more Spain delayed in accepting the terms, the more likely it became that more extensive demands would be imposed. Cambon took McKinley's words seriously and advised the Spanish government to comply. He wrote: "If the Madrid Cabinet procrastinates in its reply and does not resign itself at once to certain necessary sacrifices, such as Puerto Rico, the conditions that will be imposed on it later will be harder, and in proportion as the discussions are prolonged, circumstances will be less favorable to it."[1]

The Duque de Almodóvar, the Spanish foreign minister, was at first unwilling to accept Cambon's advice, but when he realized that McKinley was serious, he relented. On August 12, at 4:30 in the afternoon, McKinley and Cambon, acting for the Spanish government, signed a protocol that ended the hostilities. It was agreed that the formal peace conference would be held in Paris, and it was understood that the only real issue to be determined there would be the final status of the Philippines. Don Eugenio Montero Ríos, who would later head the Spanish peace commission, captured the significance of the moment: "This protocol, as one sees, made the catastrophe definite and irreparable."[2]

McKinley lost no time in selecting the members of his peace commission. The group was led by Secretary of State William Day, whose views on the Philippine question were "moderate"—meaning that he had not yet made up his mind—and included Whitelaw Reid, publisher of the *New York Tribune,* an avowed expansionist; and three senators: Cushman K. Davis (R-Minnesota), William P. Frye (R-Maine), and George Gray (D-Delaware). Davis and Frye were expansionists whereas

Gray was opposed. As secretary for the commission, McKinley named the renowned international lawyer John Bassett Moore. Obviously, the commission was stacked in favor of the expansionist point of view.

Sagasta's position was much more difficult than McKinley's because his government was on the verge of falling. Because no member of the conservative opposition would serve on the peace commission, the prime minister was forced to rely on members of his own party and professional foreign service officers. Because it was a foregone conclusion that the Spanish commission would have to give in to any and all American demands, it was virtually inevitable that Sagasta's government would collapse as soon as the peace conference ended. The members of the Spanish commission were Don Eugenio Montero Ríos, Don Buenaventura Abarazuza, Don José García y Díaz, Don Wenceslao Ramírez de Villaurrutia y Villaurrutia, and General Don Rafael Cerero y Sánez. The first three were leading members of the Liberal party, and Ramírez was minister to Belgium.

The Spanish bargaining position consisted of two major elements. First, they argued that because the Battle of Manila had taken place on August 13, the surrender was invalid because the peace protocol had been signed on August 12. Second, they argued that the Americans should assume the Cuban debt, estimated to be around $400 million. This debt represented the obligations of Cubans to Spanish creditors. The Spanish government realized that Cuban debtors would never pay; hence they proposed that the Americans assume the debt. This demand, of course, meant that Spain wanted to transfer sovereignty to the United States rather than merely give up control of the island. These proposals were contrary to American policy and therefore very unlikely to be accepted.

Meanwhile, McKinley struggled to clarify his position. The United States was not going to annex Cuba, that much was certain, but the president had not yet reached a decision on the Philippines. Opinions on both sides of the issue were persuasive, but gradually McKinley drifted toward annexation as the only rational conclusion. When he finally gave his instructions to the commission prior to their departure in September, he told them to demand—at a minimum—the cession of the island of Luzon, thus leaving open the possibility of taking the entire archipelago. "The march of events rules and over-rules human action," he told them.[3]

When the conference formally opened on October 1, it immediately became clear that the Spanish strategy was going to be to delay. Montero Ríos would attempt to draw out the proceedings interminably hoping that pressure from the international community would build sufficiently to force the Americans to make concessions. This strategy was very weak, but it was his only chance. The Americans, of course, had no intention of permitting him to succeed. Day rejected the argument that the American forces in the Philippines had no legal rights and made it clear that there was to be no discussion of substantive matters involving Cuba, Puerto Rico, and Guam. That left Montero Ríos in a very weak position and realizing this he proposed that Spain would concede to all of the American demands subject to a mutually acceptable resolution of the Philippine question.

Once they arrived in Paris the American commissioners began to debate among themselves the question of Philippine annexation. Davis, Frye, and Reid had always favored acquisition of the entire archipelago, not just Luzon, and Day had now agreed with their position. Gray still opposed taking any part of the islands. Their arguments were the same as those that would be voiced by imperialists and anti-imperialists from the fall of 1898 until the issue was decided by ratification of the Treaty of Paris in February 1899 and finally laid to rest by the outcome of the election of 1900. Day, Davis, Frye, and Reid declared that it would be dangerous to partition the islands, that it would be dishonorable to return them to Spain, and that the Filipinos would benefit immeasurably from American tutelage. Gray countered that possession of the islands would require greater military expenditures, that the American system included no provision for the subjugation of foreign populations, and that annexation was contrary to the original moral object of the war.[4]

Meanwhile, President McKinley had yet to make up his mind. He probably knew what he wanted to do, but he was reluctant to go against public opinion. Hence, he traveled about the country during October to talk and listen. He told people, "We have good money, we have ample revenues, we have unquestioned national credit, but we want new markets and as trade follows the flag, it looks very much as if we are going to have new markets."[5] He convinced himself that the people favored expansion. On October 26 he sent instructions to the commissioners ordering them to negotiate annexation of the entire Philippine archipelago. All but Gray were overjoyed. The senator believed that a terrible mistake had been made, but he felt bound to support the president and his colleagues and did so for the remainder of the conference.

When the Americans announced their intention on October 31 to take the Philippines, the Spaniards reacted with shock and dismay, as if it had never occurred to them that this would be the American course, and they immediately offered counterproposals they must have known the Americans would never accept. The first was to simply reject the idea of American annexation, the second was to propose that the United States "rent" the islands, and the third was to request a suspension of negotiations until the Spanish commission could consult their government. McKinley instructed his men to reject all these proposals.

Despite their intransigence, the Americans were aware that technically they had not conquered the Philippines. On the other hand, it had been decided that the islands were to be annexed. Therefore, the only question was how to achieve the desired result in a reasonable fashion. The solution was to offer Spain compensation. After considerable discussion it was decided to offer $20 million. Spain accepted this offer under protest, knowing there was really no other choice. The diplomats representing both parties signed the treaty on December 10, 1898, and departed with differing views. Montero Ríos wrote that the treaty was the pure expression of the immoderate demands of a conqueror, whereas Day declared that his work had brought to the country "a goodly estate indeed."[6]

In Spain, because the treaty was regarded as a disgraceful humiliation, it generated a great deal of debate. The vote in the Cortes was so close (120–118) that it was virtually meaningless, so the Queen Regent simply decreed ratification. She knew she had no other choice, but she could not protect the Liberal Ministry. Shortly after she acted Sagasta fell from power and was replaced as prime minister by the Conservative Francisco Silvela.

The treaty also generated considerable discussion in the United States. While polls seemed to show that a majority of the American people favored annexation, there was nevertheless spirited debate throughout the country and in Congress. Those who opposed ratification—the anti-imperialists—used all the arguments that had been voiced previously and also raised constitutional issues, among which was the proposition that the United States had no legal power to hold a

colony. In the Senate—where a two-thirds vote was required to ratify—
the Republicans were split, although a majority favored the treaty.
Among Democrats, on the other hand, the vast majority were opposed,
but many changed their opinion when William Jennings Bryan came
forward with the idea that the treaty should be approved and independence offered later. He wanted to end the debate to ensure that annexation would not be an issue in the forthcoming presidential election,
which he desired to contest on domestic questions. As it turned out,
fighting erupted between the Filipino and American forces at just about
the time the vote was to be taken. The outbreak of violence in addition
to Bryan's actions in all likelihood influenced the outcome, although
there is no way to prove such a conclusion. In any case, the treaty was
ratified by a two-vote margin and was proclaimed to be in effect by both
parties on April 11, 1899.

Meanwhile, President McKinley, still uncertain whether he had
made the correct decision, created another commission to go to the
Philippines and report on conditions there. To lead this group he
appointed Dr. Jacob Gould Schurman, president of Cornell University
in Ithaca, New York. Although Schurman and McKinley were friends,
Schurman was surprised by his appointment, because the president was
well aware that he opposed expansion. When he asked the president
why he had been selected, McKinley replied that he was also reluctant
but saw no alternative and was counting on Schurman for his sound
judgment. The other members of the Schurman Commission—as it
came to be known—were Professor Dean C. Worcester of the University of Michigan, author of a book on the Philippines; Charles B. Denby,
former U.S. minister to China; General Elwell S. Otis, and Admiral
George Dewey.

Otis had been named military commander in the Philippines and
was already there. By the time Schurman and the others arrived in
March 1899, war with the Filipinos had broken out, a development that
rendered their task extremely difficult. They were supposed to serve as
the eyes and ears of the U.S. government, size up the situation, mediate
factions, remove friction, and assure the Filipinos of the benevolent
intentions of the United States. Schurman set out to do his best in spite
of the difficulties. His first move was to issue a proclamation in which
he guaranteed the Filipinos civil rights, protection from exploitation,
an honest civil service, the effective administration of justice, economic

development, the construction of public works, and education. This proclamation was widely distributed, but Schurman soon learned that the insurgents rejected it.

Although he opposed expansion, Schurman concluded shortly after his arrival that the United States could not withdraw. Therefore, he sought ways to end the conflict and bestow at least some measure of home rule as soon as possible. He soon convinced himself that the only way to reach this goal was to negotiate directly with Aguinaldo, but his colleagues disagreed and the result was tension within the commission that soon led to an outright split. General Otis and the other members of the commission did not want to enter into direct negotiations with Aguinaldo because they thought it would be interpreted as a sign of weakness. They wanted to prosecute the war until the insurgents surrendered and then impose terms. After the split Schurman remained in the Philippines for a few weeks and then returned to the United States in June. At about the same time Dewey also left, but the president asked Denby and Worcester to remain and continue their investigations.

Meanwhile, Schurman toured the country, making speeches and granting interviews to the press. Because he had not officially resigned from the commission, he made certain that when he spoke it was understood that he did so on his own behalf. His message was consistent: the United States could not simply abandon the Philippines, but home rule should be granted as soon as possible. The administration did not disagree and generally endorsed his statements. Likewise, the pro-expansionist press praised him while the anti-imperialist papers criticized him harshly.

While Schurman was the focus of attention during the summer of 1899, Denby and Worcester continued their investigations as the president had requested. They gathered a great deal of information and returned to the United States late in September. A few weeks later they met with Schurman and Dewey in Washington to write their formal report. As that process went forward there was no rancor among them. They defended the American position in the Philippines, condemned Aguinaldo's uprising as unprovoked and premeditated, reaffirmed that no representative of the U.S. government had ever promised to recognize Philippine independence, and asserted firmly that the Filipinos were incapable of self-government. Their final report, published on January 31, 1900, was a massive document four volumes in length. It contained a vast amount of information that the imperialists used to argue persuasively in favor of McKinley's policies.[7]

As Schurman and his colleagues labored in Washington, war raged in the Philippines. It had begun in February when shots were exchanged between American and Filipino forces near Manila—both sides claiming that the other had fired first. It quickly developed into an all-out conflict that the McKinley administration termed an "insurrection" but that in reality was another phase of the war for independence in the Philippines. The American commander, General Otis, who was determined to prevail, went on the offensive immediately. Between March and May, when the rainy season temporarily ended the fighting, he drove the Filipinos from many of their strongholds in the lowlands into the mountains, and when they asked for a truce he refused. During this phase of the fighting many of the American troops were volunteers from the state militias whom Otis knew would soon have to be sent home. He therefore called for reinforcements, telling the president he could conquer the Philippines with 30,000 men. As it turned out there would be more than 65,000 men in the Philippines before the conflict ended, but the need for so many was not yet clear. In fact, during the spring months of 1899 Otis issued cable after cable to Washington, reassuring the president that victory was near.

Because the objective of American policy was to occupy the entire Philippine archipelago, the army had to establish bases in many locations. This was accomplished with the assistance of the navy. From these bases American forces moved out to engage the enemy and secure control of the main centers of population. Most of the fighting took place on the island of Luzon, where Aguinaldo was in personal command. At first he accommodated General Otis by engaging in conventional warfare. His poorly equipped and ill-trained forces were no match for the Americans in this type of fighting, and Otis's men under the field command of generals Arthur MacArthur and Henry L. Lawton won victory after victory. By the autumn of 1899 Otis's predictions seemed justified—the war appeared to be over, but unfortunately, this perception was incorrect. Aguinaldo's movement was nowhere near collapse. He had simply decided to change his strategy and fight a guerrilla war, believing that the Americans could not win this type of conflict. He would punish and harass them—for years, if necessary—and eventually they would give up.

This second phase of the "insurrection" was fought with unparalleled savagery on both sides. There were numerous instances of torture, assassination, wanton murder of civilians, and butchery of prisoners. For every act of terror committed by the Filipinos, the Americans responded in kind. In 1900 General Otis was recalled and General MacArthur was placed in command. He had concluded that the only way to end the fighting was to cut off the guerrillas from their sources of supply: the villages. To accomplish this he established more than 500 outposts throughout the islands near every important population center. The people in these districts were ordered to move into defined areas that could be defended by the garrisons nearby. In this way MacArthur replicated the reconcentration policy imposed by General Weyler in Cuba in 1896—the policy that had originally drawn the United States into war with Spain in the first place.

In addition to concentrating civilians in defined areas, MacArthur sent his forces into the field to harass the guerrillas. Now cut off from their sources of supply, the Filipinos could no longer resist effectively, and their military organization disintegrated. In 1901, Aguinaldo himself was captured, and soon thereafter he issued a proclamation calling for peace. All resistance gradually evaporated after that, and by 1902 the war was truly over. MacArthur's strategy appeared to have worked brilliantly and certainly he must be given credit, but two additional considerations should not be forgotten. The rebels were cut off from the outside world by the U.S. navy, and they received no help from the international community. They had requested the assistance of the Japanese, who ignored this plea. Ironically, 40 years later the Japanese would invade the islands and a combined U.S.-Filipino force under the command of Arthur MacArthur's son, Douglas, would resist them.[8]

Notes

1. Trask, *The War with Spain in 1898*, p. 430.

2. ———., p. 435.

3. H. Wayne Morgan, *William McKinley and His America* (Syracuse: Syracuse University Press, 1963), p. 435.

4. Julius W. Pratt, *Expansionists of 1898* (Chicago: Quadrangle Books, 1936), pp. 317–60.

5. Morgan, *William McKinley and His America*, p. 407.

6. ———., pp. 414–15.

7. Kenneth E. Hendrickson Jr., "Reluctant Expansionist—Jacob Gould Shurman and the Philippine Question," *Pacific Historical Review* 23, no. 4 (1967): 405–21.

8. For a thorough discussion of the Philippine "insurrection" see Brian M. Linn, *The Philippine War, 1899–1902* (Lawrence: University of Kansas Press, 2000).

CHAPTER 7

CONCLUSION: LONG-RANGE EFFECTS OF THE SPANISH-AMERICAN WAR

The Spanish-American War produced a revolutionary change in U.S. foreign policy, the effects of which reverberated throughout the twentieth century. America went to war in 1898 with no plans for conquest or territorial expansion, but before the year was out the nation possessed an empire. The American people supported the war at the beginning because they viewed it as a humanitarian crusade to save the Cubans from the ravages of Spanish brutality. By the end of the war the majority of Americans saw its outcome as clear evidence of the inevitability of Manifest Destiny.

The outcome in the Philippines accurately reflects the change in attitude that occurred during the summer of 1898. The key, of course, was Dewey's victory in the Battle of Manila Bay. Historians disagree about the purpose of Dewey's mission. Some believe his goal was simply to neutralize the Spanish Pacific Squadron, whereas others are convinced it was the first step in a strategy of conquest. In any case, once Dewey destroyed the Spanish fleet in Manila Bay, the United States faced the reality that difficult decisions had to be made. As the smoke of controversy cleared away, it became obvious that only one viable course of action was open to McKinley's government. Perhaps he received a revelation from God and perhaps he did not, but the fact remains that given the circumstances McKinley could not withdraw. That would be dishonorable and damaging to American interests. Of course, the matter was complicated by the presence of Aguinaldo and his forces.

Aguinaldo never deviated from the claim that he was persuaded to return to the islands to fight for independence with American assistance, and that he had been betrayed. At best, our knowledge of his relationship with Dewey and other Americans in the Far East is cloudy and the truth will probably never be known, but nevertheless it would have been foolhardy for the Americans to withdraw and leave the Philippines open to conquest by another power. Even though the Philippines never served as the steppingstone to China that some envisioned, that possibility certainly existed, and to abandon it would have subjected McKinley to justifiably harsh criticism.[1]

The acquisition of the Philippines necessitated the development of two policies in the early twentieth century. The first involved the administration of the Philippines themselves and the second concerned relations with other powers that had interests in the Far East. With respect to the first policy, American rule began, of course, with military occupation, under General Elwell S. Otis and then General Arthur MacArthur. Military rule was followed by the creation of an administrative commission headed by William H. Taft. About the time Taft was appointed, Congress passed the Spooner Amendment to the Military Appropriations Bill, a measure that essentially conferred dictatorial powers upon the president. McKinley delegated much of this authority to Taft, who set out to train the Filipinos in the art of self-government and prepare them for autonomy and eventual independence.

The Organic Act,[2] passed late in 1902, paved the way for the election of a Filipino assembly. It also declared the island residents to be citizens of the Philippines with the rights conferred by the U.S. Constitution. The next step in the evolution of Philippine independence was the Jones Act,[3] passed by Congress in 1916. It affirmed that it had always been the policy of the United States to grant independence as soon as possible, and it provided for the creation of an elected legislature consisting of a house and a senate. The precise amount of autonomy enjoyed by the Filipinos varied over the next two decades, but finally, in 1934, the McDuffie-Tydings Act[4] provided for a 10-year probationary period, following which independence would be conferred. Independence was delayed by World War II, but on July 4, 1946, the Philippines finally became an independent republic.[5]

The acquisition of the Philippines and other island possessions in the Pacific triggered the changes in American foreign policy in the Far

East that were reflected in the Open Door policy. The Open Door was a major shift and was very significant. In March 1898, the United States declined to join Great Britain in a bilateral statement affirming the rights of all nations to trade and invest in China on an equal basis. This decision reflected the Monroe Doctrine of 1823, in which the United States announced that she would not meddle in the affairs of the Eastern Hemisphere and expected other nations not to meddle in the affairs of the Western Hemisphere. Later, in 1898, with the acquisition of the Philippines, conditions had changed. Secretary of State John Hay sent a note to all the major powers with interests in the Far East asking them to agree to precisely the same terms. Even though all answered equivocally, Hay announced publicly that all had agreed, and thus the Open Door policy was born. It committed the United States to the protection of equal opportunity for all nations to trade and invest in China and to the preservation of the territorial and administrative integrity of China. Among the numerous significant long-range results of this policy shift, perhaps the most important was the relationship with Japan, a relationship that was significantly affected by the activities of the Russians.[6]

In the days following the announcement of the Open Door, all parties viewed the behavior of the Russians with growing concern. They had become very aggressive in Manchuria and even developed an interest in Korea. In 1902, the British sought to neutralize possible Russian aggression by making an alliance with Japan, following which the Japanese launched military and naval action against the Russians in what became known as the Russo-Japanese War (1904–1905). Officially, America was neutral in this conflict but made little attempt to disguise pro-Japanese sympathies. Hence, when the Japanese—who were winning the war, though at great cost—secretly asked Theodore Roosevelt to mediate a settlement, he agreed. Russia, convulsed by a revolution in 1905, also agreed, and Roosevelt invited both parties to a peace conference in the United States. The resulting Treaty of Portsmouth in 1905[7] ended the war and Theodore Roosevelt won a Nobel Peace Prize, but it angered the Japanese, who had hoped for better terms, including territorial adjustments and reparations. From that point on U.S. relations with Japan began to deteriorate.

Even before the terms of the Treaty of Portsmouth were finalized, Secretary of War William Howard Taft met with Japanese prime minister Katsura and concluded an agreement by which the United States promised not to interfere with Japanese activities in Korea and the Japanese promised they had no designs on the Philippines. The Taft-Katsura Agreement (July 29, 1905)[8] was not in accord with the Open Door and was kept secret for many years. Moreover, it did not promote greater friendship between the two nations. Japanese nationalists continued to be upset over the Treaty of Portsmouth and were even more disturbed by the treatment of Japanese immigrants in the western United States. The immigration problem was especially acute in California, where there were many unskilled Japanese immigrants willing to work for very low pay. An effort in Congress aimed at Japanese exclusion failed in 1906, but in the same year city officials in San Francisco segregated Asians and white students in the public schools. This action infuriated the Japanese, who demanded satisfaction. Roosevelt could not force local officials to recant, but he was able to persuade them to do so in exchange for a promise by the Japanese government to deny passports to laborers.

Fearful that the Japanese might interpret his actions as a sign of weakness, Roosevelt decided to send the American fleet on an around-the-world tour designed to signal American strength. The trip received an enormous amount of publicity and on the surface appeared to promote peace. Behind the scenes, however, the Japanese resented this blatant show of force and redoubled their efforts to strengthen their navy. That they intended eventually to dominate the Far East should by this time have been patently clear.

Even before the voyage of the "Great White Fleet" was completed, another secret accord cemented the relationship between the two nations. The Root-Takahira Agreement of 1908[9] provided that both nations would support the status quo in the Pacific, would not interfere with each other's possessions, and would support the independence of China. On the surface this agreement was a step designed to promote peace, but in fact it accomplished little.[10] Later, in 1914, when a Japanese business syndicate sought to acquire a site on Magdalena Bay in lower California, the outcry in the United States was so intense that the plan had to be dropped. This controversy in turn led to the introduction of the Lodge Corollary to the Monroe Doctrine. Submitted to the Senate by Henry Cabot Lodge, this declaration provided that the acquisition of any harbor or place in the Western Hemisphere that might be used for military or naval purposes by a non-American government would be viewed as a threat. The Lodge Corollary was hailed as a giant step forward in the United States but caused even greater resentment in Japan.[11] From this time forward Japan did everything possible to strengthen her position in the Far East. By the 1930s these policies had matured to outright aggression in China and Southeast Asia, making war between the United States and Japan almost inevitable. Hostilities erupted in late 1941 when the Japanese attempted to destroy the American fleet at Pearl Harbor and then launched an invasion of the Philippines. The historical sources of this conflict can be tied directly to the events of 1898.

The Spanish-American War also produced long-term consequences in the Caribbean. At the outset the war was fought to secure freedom for the Cubans, not to acquire new territory in the Western Hemisphere. The Teller amendment clearly stated that Cuba would not be annexed, but by the end of hostilities there in July it was obvious that conditions precluded immediate withdrawal. Fear of counterrevolution; the possibility that other powers might intervene; the absence of any experience in self-government; and the high rates of poverty, illiteracy, and disease combined to require some form of American control. Hence the Cubans, like the Filipinos, found themselves living under military rule rather than enjoying a newfound independence. Many were outraged, but in the long run the benefits of occupation were substantial. The Americans built roads; established schools; and worked hard to eradicate disease, especially yellow fever. In 1900 the military governor, Colonel Leonard Wood, concluded that the Cubans were ready for self-government and allowed them to convene an assembly that drew up a proposed framework of government. Because the War Department rejected these proposals, Wood and Secretary of War Elihu Root prepared a rider to the Military Appropriation Bill of 1901 that came to be known as the Platt Amendment.[12] This document was incorporated into a treaty between the United States and Cuba in 1903 and became the basis of the relationship between Cuba and the United States for the next three decades. It limited Cuban sovereignty and for all practical purposes made Cuba a protectorate of the United States. Specifically, the Platt Amendment required that Cuba make no treaties without U.S. approval, limit its debt, allow U.S. military intervention whenever necessary, and allow the United States to establish military or naval bases in Cuban territory.[13]

The United States abrogated the Platt Amendment in 1929, but even so, relations between the United States and Cuba remained close for another 30 years. During that period most Cuban governments were corrupt, incompetent, or both, and the last one, presided over by Fulencio Batista, was overthrown in a revolt led by Fidel Castro in 1959. Castro soon allied himself with the Soviet Union and has ruled Cuba ever since. Cuba came to be almost totally reliant on the USSR, and when that "evil empire" collapsed in 1989, the Cuban economy cratered. Today, bereft of Russian aid and hamstrung by an American boycott, the Cuban economy is in a state of collapse.[14]

By the terms of the Treaty of Paris the United States gained permanent possession of Puerto Rico and Congress was granted the power to determine the political status of the inhabitants. Thus American policy in Puerto Rico differed considerably from that in Cuba. After the conquest the island was administered by the military until in 1900 Congress passed the Foraker Act,[15] which established civil government. Under this law the inhabitants of the island were designated "citizens of Puerto Rico" and did not enjoy all the privileges of United States citizenship. For example, the governor was an appointed American, they could not elect the members of the upper house in the legislature, and they had no voting representatives in Congress. This system remained in effect until 1917, when Congress passed the Jones Act, or the Puerto Rican Organic Act.[16] This law made Puerto Rico a territory of the United States and the people American citizens with all the privileges of the Bill of Rights except trial by jury. In 1952 Puerto Rico was designated a commonwealth, although little else was changed. Puerto Ricans are American citizens, can immigrate freely, and may serve in the military. They can vote for their own governor and legislature, but not for president or for a voting member of Congress. The vast majority of Puerto Ricans are satisfied with this arrangement, but there are a few advocates of independence (including some who are prepared to resort to violence), and others who would like statehood. Neither of these objectives is likely to be achieved any time soon simply because most people do not care. Although many people have always regarded colonial rule as un-American, and although the constitutional status of Puerto Rico remains unclear, its commonwealth status will undoubtedly continue indefinitely.[17]

The acquisition of these new territories generated major questions of political theory and constitutional law as well as mundane administrative issues. Throughout American history, as territory was acquired it was always assumed that such territory was destined to be admitted to the union. In the minds of many Americans, however, that assumption was invalid when applied to the far-flung island possessions. For them it was inconceivable that the inhabitants of these islands should ever become full-fledged citizens of equal states. For other Americans the very idea of the United States having colonies and governing subject peoples on a permanent basis was abhorrent. The question to be answered was, "To what extent does the Constitution apply to the inhabitants of the newly acquired territories: in part, in total, or not all?" The answer came in the form of two Supreme Court decisions, the so-called Insular Cases, of 1901. In *DeLima* v. *Bidwell* (182-US1) the question was whether goods imported from Puerto Rico were subject to a tariff. In a 5–4 decision the court ruled that Puerto Rico was not a foreign country and that therefore duties could not be collected. Later in the year came the case of *Downes* v. *Bidwell*. In the previous decision the Court had not made it clear whether Congress could impose special duties on goods imported from the islands. As a result U.S. sugar interests were able to persuade Congress to place a special 15 percent tax on imports from Puerto Rico. The question in *Downes* v. *Bidwell* (182 US244) was whether this special tax violated the constitutional provision that all duties must be uniform throughout the nation. In its ruling the court decreed that the Constitution did not automatically follow the flag but was extended to outlying territories only if Congress so ordered. This decision confirmed the view of the imperialists that the United States could extend its rule over any people regarded as inferior without any requirement to grant them the full rights of citizenship. Technically and legally the issue was resolved, but ethically it continued to generate debate for decades to come.[18]

The outcome of the Spanish-American War also generated a more aggressive foreign policy in the Caribbean. The Platt Amendment authorized American military intervention in Cuba under certain circumstances, and in 1906,when civil war threatened the island, American troops reestablished military rule, remaining until 1909. Their withdrawal, however, did not bring an end to American domination because the Platt Amendment remained in effect.

The most dramatic expression of the new American policy can be seen in the case of the Panama Canal. The desirability of an isthmian canal had been discussed throughout the nineteenth century, but the Spanish-American War provided dramatic evidence of the need to proceed without further delay. The voyage of the *Oregon* and the acquisition of the Pacific islands demonstrated the need to link the two oceans if the new possessions were to be adequately protected. But once the decision to go ahead was made, numerous obstacles were still to be overcome. One was an old agreement with Britain stipulating that neither country would build, fortify, or operate an isthmian canal without the consent of the other. Another was the question of precisely where to put the canal.

The problem with the British was resolved by amicable negotiations, but the question of location was complicated. A French company had attempted to build a canal through Panama, then a part of Columbia, in the 1880s. The attempt failed, but the company still owned the rights to the site. Many people, including Theodore Roosevelt, favored the Panama route but were unwilling to pay the French company the exorbitant $109 million fee it was demanding to relinquish its rights. The other possible route lay through Nicaragua, and it was all but approved when simultaneously the French company lowered its demands to $40 million and advocates of the Panama route pointed out that there were volcanoes in Nicaragua. The U.S. government then accepted the Panama route.

Because Panama was a part of Colombia, permission had to be requested from that country. Secretary of State John Hay negotiated an agreement with the Colombian minister to pay his government $10 million plus $250,000 a year to lease a strip of land six miles wide across the isthmus.[19] The U.S. Congress approved the pact, but the Colombian government did not because it was hoping for a better deal. Roosevelt was infuriated and so were the Panamanians, who looked forward to the great economic benefits the canal would bring them, and with covert assistance from the United States they declared independence. There was no resistance from the Colombian military, whose leaders in Panama were bribed, and Enrique Bunau-Varilla, a representative of the French Canal Company, became foreign minister of the new republic. He then negotiated a treaty with the United States granting a lease in perpetuity and permission to build the canal.[20] Theodore Roosevelt regarded this treaty as one of his greatest achievements. Construction began at once, and the canal opened in 1914.

The Panama Canal not only had a profound effect on naval strategy and commercial activity but also gave the United States another asset to defend in the Caribbean. This obligation made an aggressive policy there even more important because no potentially hostile foreign power could be allowed to gain a foothold anywhere near this vital waterway, and no small nation could be allowed to fall into such a state of disorder or financial instability as to provoke foreign intervention. For Theodore Roosevelt these conditions meant that a readiness to use force should be a vital element of foreign policy, and everyone should understand that.[21]

Roosevelt's policy decisions early in the twentieth century were triggered by an incident involving Venezuela in 1902. Venezuela had massive debts to European creditors and was not paying. The creditors appealed to their governments for assistance and in December 1902 the British, German, and Italian navies established a blockade. At first Roosevelt did not object, but he became concerned when the Europeans bombarded the Venezuelan coast. Eventually the dispute was submitted to arbitration, to which the European governments agreed when they began to realize that American public opinion was becoming hostile.

For his part, Roosevelt resolved never to allow European intervention to happen again, and when similar circumstances arose in the Dominican Republic the next year, his response was very different. Rather than allow the French and Italians to send armed forces, Roosevelt announced that the United States would take over the administration of Dominican finances. Then, in his annual message to Congress delivered in early 1904, Roosevelt declared that any time a country in the Western Hemisphere could not or would not meet its obligations, the United States would intervene rather than allow intervention by a European power. This policy came to be known as the Roosevelt Corollary to the Monroe Doctrine. In the Dominican Republic the financial arrangement continued for several years until deteriorating conditions in 1911 required the sending of troops. Thus the Roosevelt Corollary came to have two elements: financial control and military intervention, if necessary.[22]

In subsequent administrations this policy came to be known as "Dollar Diplomacy," and before World War I it was applied in Honduras, Nicaragua, and Haiti in addition to the Dominican Republic. It worked like this: If a small nation with financial problems was threatened with European intervention, the U.S. government would persuade private bankers to lend money to the bankrupt state. Because the bankers would demand safeguards for the loans, American administrators and troops would be dispatched. Special elections would produce victory for a local politician friendly to the United States. He would then grant concessions to American investors who would reap enormous profits. The justification for such actions was the need to safeguard the Panama Canal, but in reality it was a form of economic imperialism the origins of which could be traced back to conditions generated by the outcome of the war with Spain. This policy continued until the outbreak of World War II and did little to promote hemispheric friendship and solidarity.[23]

Notes

1. Leech, *In the Days of McKinley*, pp. 323–28, 339–41, 353–59.

2. *Statutes at Large* 32 (1903): pp. 691–712.

3. *Statutes at Large* 39-1 (1917): pp. 545–56.

4. *Statutes at Large* 48 (1934): pp. 456–65.

5. Leech, *In the Days of McKinley*, pp. 568–69.

6. Kenton J. Clymer, *John Hay: The Gentleman as Diplomat* (Ann Arbor: University of Michigan Press, 1975), pp. 146–47, 151, 154–55.

7. For the "Treaty of Portsmouth," see Sydney Tyler, *The Japan-Russia War* (Harrisburg, Penn.: Minister Company), pp. 564–68.

8. For the "Taft-Katsura Agreement" see U.S. Department of State, *Papers Relating to the Foreign Relations in the United States, 1908* (Washington, D.C.: U S Government Printing Office, 1912), pp. 510–12.

9. For the "Root-Takahira Agreement" see U.S. Department of State, *Papers Relating to the Foreign Relations of the United States, 1908* (Washington, D.C.: U.S. Government Printing Office, 1912), pp. 510–12.

10. Alexander De Conde, *A History of American Foreign Policy* (New York: Charles Scribner's Sons, 1963), pp. 367–73.

11. ———., pp. 425–26.

12. For the *Platt Amendment* see *Statutes at Large* 31-2 (1901): pp. 897–98.

13. Morgan, *William McKinley and His America*, pp. 447–49.

14. For details concerning the relationship between the United States and Cuba throughout the twentieth century, see Samuel Flagg Bemises's *A Diplomatic History of the United States*, 5th ed. (New York: Holt, Rinehart and Winston, 1965), pp. 464, 468, 473, 503–5, 506–7, 572, 990–94. See also Pérez Jr., *Cuba and the United States*; Jaine Suchliki, *Cuba from Columbus to Cortez* (New York: Charles Scribner's Sons, 1974), pp. 74–224; Mark T. Gilderhus,

The Second Century: U.S. Latin-American Relations Since 1889 (Wilmington, Del.: Scholarly Resources, 2000), pp. 163–247.

15. For the *Foraker Act* see *Statutes at Large* 31-1 (1900): pp. 77–86.

16. For the *Jones Act* see *Statutes at Large* 39 (1917): pp. 951–68.

17. For a thorough discussion of U.S. relations with Puerto Rico see Roland J. Perusse, *The United States and Puerto Rico: The Struggle for Equality* (Malabar, Fla.: Robert E. Krieger, 1990).

18. Alfred H. Kelley and Winfred A. Harbison, *The American Constitution: Its Origins and Development,* 3d ed. (New York: Norton, 1963), pp. 577–78.

19. This is the "Hay-Herrán Treaty." See D. C. Miner, *The Fight for the Panama Route: The Story of the Spooner Act and the Hay-Herrán Treaty* (New York: Octagon Books, 1971), pp. 413–26.

20. This is the "Hay-Buneau-Varilla Treaty." See Charles I. Blevans, ed., *Treaties and Other International Organizations of the United States of America, 1776–1949,* vol. 10 (Washington, D.C.: U.S. Government Printing Office, 1974), pp. 665–72.

21. William H. Harbaugh, *Power and Responsibility: The Life and Times of Theodore Roosevelt* (New York: Farrar, Straus, and Cudahy, 1961), pp. 198–200; 206–09; 398–99; 464–65.

22. ———., pp. 191–97.

23. De Conde, *A History of American Foreign Policy,* pp. 422–27.

Battleship USS *Maine* explodes in Havana Harbor on the night of February 15, 1898. Courtesy of the Library of Congress.

The Battle of Manila Bay. The Spanish Squadron under the command of Admiral Patricio Montojo is destroyed by Commodore George Dewey. Courtesy of the Library of Congress.

Transports in Tampa Bay awaiting departure, June 1898. Courtesy of the Library of Congress.

American forces landing unopposed at Daiquiri on the southern coast of Cuba. Courtesy of the Library of Congress.

Generals Nelson Miles, William Shafter, and Joseph Wheeler in conference.
Courtesy of the Library of Congress.

The assault on Spanish defenses at El Caney, July 1, 1898. Courtesy of the Library of Congress.

American troops under fire at the base of San Juan Hill prior to the assault on July 1, 1898. Courtesy of the Library of Congress.

Theodore Roosevelt and the Rough Riders atop Kettle Hill, July 1, 1898. Courtesy of the Library of Congress.

The Spanish Squadron under the command of Admiral Pascual Cervera is destroyed by American warships under the command of admirals William Sampson and Winfield Scott Schley. Courtesy of the Library of Congress.

Members of the Twentieth Kansas Volunteers returning to camp from battle in the Philippines. Courtesy of the Library of Congress.

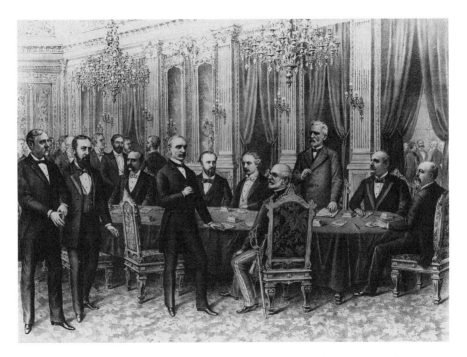

The representatives of the United States and Spain at the peace conference in Paris. Courtesy of the Library of Congress.

President William McKinley. Courtesy of the Library of Congress.

BIOGRAPHICAL SKETCHES: SIGNIFICANT PERSONS IN THE SPANISH - AMERICAN WAR

Emilo Aguinaldo y Famy, 1869–1964

Aguinaldo was born at Cavite on the island of Luzon. His father was active in local affairs and was mayor of Cavite Viejo at the time of his death in 1878. Later, in 1895, Aguinaldo would hold the same position. That same year he joined the Katipunan. The name of this nationalist organization is a word in the Tagalog language that means "society of the sons of the people." The Katipunan was founded in 1892 by Andrés Bonifacio. It appealed mostly to the lower strata of society and advocated violent revolution. In 1896 Bonifacio launched a revolt in which Aguinaldo played a leading role. He led the insurgent forces in Cavite and in November his forces inflicted a major defeat on the Spaniards. This led to Aguinaldo's rapid rise to power within the organization.

In 1897 a struggle for power erupted among the rebels. Aguinaldo overthrew Bonifacio, had him executed, and seized control of the revolution for himself. Not able to wage conventional warfare against the Spaniards, he retreated into the hills, and from there he conducted a guerrilla campaign. At the same time he published his demands:

1. Expulsion of the Spanish friars and division of the property among the Spanish and Filipino secular clergy
2. Autonomy, freedom of the press, and political toleration
3. Equal pay for equal work
4. Return of expropriated land to the owners
5. Legal reforms leading to equitable treatment for Filipinos

Unable to prevail by force, Aguinaldo made a deal with the Spanish governor general, Fernando Primo de Rivera, by which he agreed to be banished to Hong Kong in exchange for 800,000 Mexican pesos. Rivera also agreed to institute certain moderate reforms, but he never paid all the money and there were no reforms. Hence, by 1878 Aguinaldo was looking for ways to return home and resurrect the revolution.

Meanwhile, insurgent representatives in Hong Kong had proposed an alliance with the United States. This was rebuffed, but in early 1898 Aguinaldo became involved. He later claimed that in a series of conferences with American naval officers he was encouraged to return to the Philippines and lead an attack against the Spaniards with American assistance. There is no evidence to support this claim.

Aguinaldo left for Europe on April 7, 1898, but on the April 21 his ship called at Singapore, and there he met with U.S. consul general E. S. Pratt, who urged him to return to Hong Kong but made no commitment on behalf of his government. Aguinaldo later claimed that Pratt committed the United States to Philippine independence and an American protectorate. Commodore Dewey later testified that he wanted Aguinaldo to return to Hong Kong to "quiet the Filipinos." "They were bothering me," he said. There was and there remains much controversy about what actually happened and what agreements were reached, but in any case one of Dewey's ships transported Aguinaldo to the islands. He arrived on May 19 and immediately called forth his forces to do battle with the Spaniards. He later claimed that Dewey had promised him that the United States supported Philippine independence. Dewey denied the claim, but the United States did supply arms and ammunition to Aguinaldo's force of almost 12,000 men.

Aguinaldo began operations against the Spanish forces in and around Manila in late May. Soon, an American force led by General Thomas M. Anderson arrived, but there was little cooperation between the Americans and Aguinaldo's forces. When General Wesley Merritt took command in July he decided to fight the Spaniards without any regard for the Filipinos. He behaved as though they were not there. For all practical purposes Merritt ordered Aguinaldo to stay out of his way, and Aguinaldo concluded that he had been betrayed.

The Filipinos were not involved in the peace negotiations between the United States and Spain, and for many weeks an uneasy truce prevailed between the insurgents and the Americans in the vicinity of Manila. The truce ended on the night of February 4, 1899, when Private William Grayson fired at a group of Filipinos approaching his position. Shooting soon spread all along the 10-mile line between the two forces and resulted in hundreds of casualties. The Philippine Insurrection had begun.

As the fighting continued the superior American forces quickly pushed the Filipinos farther back into the interior of the island of Luzon. Just as he had done earlier against the Spaniards, Aguinaldo resorted to guerrilla tactics; a savage conflict followed that lasted for three years and featured unspeakable atrocities committed by both sides. Finally, in March 1902 Aguinaldo was captured and all resistance by the Filipinos gradually ended. President Roosevelt issued an official proclamation of peace on July 4, 1902, and also conferred amnesty on all those who had participated in the rebellion. Aguinaldo swore allegiance to the United States and retired from public life. He died at an advanced age in 1964, having lived long enough to see his dream of Philippine independence come true in 1946.

Russell A. Alger, 1836–1907

Alger was born in Lafayette, Ohio. Although orphaned at an early age, he supported himself and two young siblings and was able to get an education. In 1857 he was admitted to the bar in Ohio but soon moved to Michigan, where he became a successful lawyer. He fought in the Civil War, retiring as a major general, and afterward pursued a lucrative career in business and politics. From 1885 to 1886 he served as governor of his state.

When William McKinley ran for president in 1896, Alger supported him vigorously and was rewarded with a position in the cabinet as secretary of war. An affable yet egotistical man, Alger actually possessed little administrative ability, and his tenure was just short of disastrous. He failed to take sufficient advantage of the fifty million dollar bill, and he grossly underestimated the difficulties of making a large volunteer army combat ready in a short time. His problems were not all of his own making, however. The War Department over which he presided was a cumbersome organization made up of 10 bureaus, each presided over by a brigadier general. Alger had to deal with all of them. Moreover, in 1898 the U.S. Army was only 28,000 strong and could not possibly fight a war successfully without volunteers. Alger asked for 60,000 volunteers, but the president actually called for 125,000. The large number of soldiers led to many difficulties in organizing and equipping the force.

In spite of these problems, pressure to launch an attack in Cuba became intense, and on May 8, 1898, Alger ordered General Nelson A. Miles to lead 70,000 troops to Cuba and capture Havana. This order was ridiculous, of course, because American forces were not ready to launch an invasion. Thus Alger had to back down, and as a result he appeared incompetent. This incident clouded his reputation from then on, even though some of his decisions demonstrated more lucid thinking.

Throughout the war Alger also had problems with interservice rivalries. Not only was his relationship with Secretary of Navy Long generally unsatisfactory, but he was also never able to bring about any level of cooperation between the army and the navy that might have made the conduct of the war more effective. Even the successful outcome of the war brought Alger no accolades. On the contrary, McKinley formed a blue-ribbon commission headed by railroad tycoon Grenville Dodge to investigate charges of corruption and incompetence. These charges stemmed from allegations by Miles that Alger had allowed meat packers to send the army canned beef that was unfit for human consumption and that this incident reflected the generally low level of Alger's overall performance. The commission absolved the secretary of all charges but nevertheless concluded that his performance demonstrated an inability to grasp the situation in a way that was essential to the highest efficiency and discipline of the army.

On August 1, 1899, Alger resigned from the cabinet and retired to his home state of Michigan, where he wrote a book entitled *The Spanish-American War* in which he defended his actions. In 1902, the Michigan legislature appointed him to fill a vacancy in the U.S. Senate and the next year he was elected to a full term. He died in office on January 24, 1907.

Admiral Pascual Cervera y Topete, 1839–1909

Born in Medina Sidonia, Cadiz, in 1839, Cervera entered the naval academy of San Fernando in 1852 at age 13. This was the beginning of a long and distinguished career.

By 1898, when war with the United States was imminent, Cervera commanded the Spanish squadron based at Cadiz. Among the nation's most respected naval officers, he was also unalterably opposed to fighting a war far from home. But Cervera also knew that national honor would require a show of force in the event of war with the Americans.

The admiral attempted to convince Segismundo Bermejo, the Spanish minister of marine, that the United States was technically superior and that Spain lacked sufficient coal, ammunition, and provisions to fight, but he was unsuccessful. In early April he was ordered to take his fleet to the Cape Verde Islands and a few weeks later was told to head for the West Indies. Realizing that he was being sent on a suicide mission, Cervera nevertheless did as he was told. Eventually, on May 19, the Spanish squadron reached Santiago and slipped into the harbor. By this time Cervera's force consisted of seven ships, none of which was fit to battle any American cruiser or battleship. Nevertheless, the loyalists in Santiago were overjoyed. They mistakenly believed that Cervera's decrepit force could save them from the Americans.

It took several days for the Americans to determine the exact location of Cervera's squadron, and it was not until May 29 that the U.S. navy blockaded the entrance to Santiago Bay. In the meantime Cervera could have escaped, but political pressure prevented him from doing so. Once the blockade began, Cervera was trapped.

The climactic naval engagement of the Spanish-American War took place on the morning of Sunday, July 3, 1898. Cervera was ordered to leave the harbor and fight it out with the American admiral William T. Sampson in order to preserve Spanish honor. He was enraged by an order he considered nothing short of madness, but he obeyed.

Cervera believed that his best chance, small as it was, was to flee the harbor on a Sunday morning while the Americans held captains' inspection. So, at 9:30 A.M. on Sunday, July 3, the Spanish vessels emerged from the harbor in single file. Within a short time all of Cervera's ships were sunk, run aground, or otherwise put out of action. There was catastrophic loss of life among his crews and Cervera himself was captured, but he won the admiration of his enemies for his daring and courage. He was released from captivity in September 1898 and returned to Spain, where he continued to serve the crown until his retirement. He died at Puerto Real, Spain, in 1909.

Admiral George Dewey, 1837–1917

Dewey commanded the U.S. squadron in the Pacific that attacked and destroyed the Spanish force in Manila Bay on May 1, 1898. Not only was this the first action of the Spanish-American War, but more importantly, it also signaled the emergence of the United States as a world-class naval power and made the commodore a national hero.

George Dewey was born in Montpelier, Vermont, in 1837 into a family that had settled in New England early in the seventeenth century. His mother, Mary Perrin Dewey, died when he was five years old and he was raised by his father, Dr. Julius Dewey, whom he later credited for his success in life. In 1854 young George was appointed to the U.S. Naval Academy and graduated four years later fifth in his class. This marked the beginning of a naval career that would span 62 years.

Before the outbreak of the Civil War Dewey served on the steam frigate *Wabash*, which cruised in the Mediterranean Sea. During the Civil War he participated in several major battles, including the attacks on New Orleans in 1862, Port Hudson in 1864, and Port Fisher in 1865. Much of the time he was under the command of the great David Farragut, who greatly influenced him. In the years following the Civil War Dewey served in various capacities: he was commander of the sloop-of-war *Narragansett* (1870–75), naval secretary of the Light House Board in Washington (1875–82), and commander of the sloop *Juniata* (1882–84). During this third tour he became seriously ill with typhoid fever and an abscessed liver and nearly died.

In 1884 Dewey was promoted to captain and then given command of the cruiser *Pensacola*. In 1889, he was named chief of the Bureau of Equipment in Washington, a position that gave him the opportunity to oversee the development and construction of America's new cruisers and battleships. After six years in this position he was named president of the Board of Inspection and Survey. This was in October 1895, when five battleships and numerous small craft were near completion. Dewey's job was to ensure that all the vessels were properly built and conformed to all specifications.

In November 1897, now holding the rank of commodore, Dewey was given command of the Asiatic Squadron. Relations with Spain were already tense, and Dewey knew that if war came the Philippines would undoubtedly be his target. Therefore, he undertook an in-depth study of the islands, their people, and their geography. He also put his ships and crews through a period of rigorous training and acquired all the provisions and ammunition he thought necessary. From February until April 1898, he remained on station at Hong Kong. During that time he received an order from Assistant Secretary of the Navy Theodore Roosevelt to be prepared to attack the Spanish fleet at Manila immediately should war break out between the United States and Spain.

On April 26, 1898, Dewey was informed that war had been declared and set sail at once. He found the Spanish fleet, consisting of six ships, at anchor in Manila Bay on the night of April 30 and attacked them at dawn the following day. Neither the return fire from the Spanish ships nor their shore batteries were effective and by noon Dewey had destroyed the Spanish force. All the Spanish ships were either sunk or destroyed and the Spanish suffered nearly 400 casualties. Only eight Americans were injured and none killed.

Dewey remained in Pacific waters for about a year after the battle. When he finally returned home he received a hero's welcome. There were parades in New York and other cities, and a gratified government presented the commodore with a house in Washington. Some people even suggested that he should run for president. His pride and ego were stimulated by this idea and on April 4, 1900, he issued a public statement saying, "Since studying this subject I am convinced the office of president is not such a very difficult one to fill." This remark made Dewey look ridiculous, but it should not have. It was very much in character. Throughout his life he had studied and prepared thoroughly for every challenge and had overcome them all. In any case, his remark mattered little, for neither major party gave him any consideration.

Dewey was appointed president of the General Board of the Navy Department in 1900 and served in this office until his death. His hard work and prestige gave the board much more power and influence than it would otherwise have enjoyed. Working regularly until the very end despite the onset of serious physical problems, Dewey died in Washington on January 16, 1917.

Enrique Dupuy de Lôme, 1851–1904

Dupuy de Lôme served as the Spanish minister to the United States from 1892 until February 1898. He was generally well respected until the onslaught of the Cuban crisis caused his relationship with William McKinley, who became president in March 1897, to deteriorate. He found himself under mounting pressure to intervene in Cuba and gave clear indications that he intended to alter the policies of his predecessor, Grover Cleveland. One of these was his decision to send the battleship *Maine* to Havana as a symbol of American power and determination to protect American interests. Secretary of State William R. Day informed Dupuy de Lôme of the president's intentions, and the ambassador gave his approval. On the surface Dupuy de Lôme attempted to convey an image of cordiality but in fact he was enraged. He disapproved of the policy of the Sagasta government that conferred autonomy on Cuba and he had little respect for McKinley. He feared that events were hurtling out of control and might lead to war. Moreover, he believed that McKinley was a weak, waffling politician who lacked the strength of character necessary to preserve peace. The minister confided his fears to a friend in Havana in a letter written in December 1897. This letter was stolen and eventually found its way into the hands of the Cuban junta in New York. The Cubans in turn gave it to William Randolph Hearst, who published it in his newspaper, the *New York Journal*. Papers all over the country published similar stories, resulting in an immediate outpouring of public indignation. Dupuy de Lôme resigned and the Spanish government apologized, but it was too late. A few days later the *Maine* blew up and war became inevitable.

Máximo Gómez y Báez, 1836–1905

Gómez was born in Santo Domingo and migrated to Cuba in 1865, where he soon became involved in revolutionary activity. He participated in the Ten Years' War (1868–1878) but was not surprised when it failed to produce Cuban independence.

In 1895 José Martí, leader of a new independence movement, asked Gómez to command his military forces. Gómez accepted and began guerrilla action against the Spaniards in the eastern provinces of Cuba. The Spanish army, even though it outnumbered Gómez's forces nearly 10 to 1, could not effectively combat his hit-and-run tactics. Hence, even though Gómez had inadequate supplies and ammunition, he fought on. When Spanish prime minister Antonio Cánovas del Castillo offered the Cubans autonomy, hoping to disarm the revolution in that way, Gómez refused to be deterred. He believed that exerting unending military pressure on Spain over a long time could win independence.

Gómez hoped for American intervention and expected to fight alongside the Americans, but he was troubled by the racism and arrogance the Americans exhibited when they arrived, and he discovered they did not particularly want to fight jointly with his forces. Nevertheless, he supported a policy of accommodation with the United States. When hostilities ended on August 12, 1898, Gómez agreed to disband his forces. He then retired from public life and devoted himself to writing articles that warned his countrymen of America's intention to exert permanent control over Cuba. He rejected an invitation to run for president of Cuba in 1900 and lived in retirement in Havana until his death in 1906.

John Davis Long, 1838–1915

Born in Buckfield, Oxford County, Maine, in 1838, Long received his primary and secondary education there and went on to graduate from Harvard in 1857. He attended law school and was admitted to the bar in 1861. He began his practice in Maine, then moved to Massachusetts permanently in 1869. Long was active in politics and was a member of the Massachusetts House of Representatives (1875–1878), where he served as Speaker. He was elected lieutenant governor in 1879 and governor in 1880. From 1885 to 1889 he served in Congress but did not run for reelection in 1888. Instead, he returned to Boston to revive his law practice. However, he remained active in Republican Party affairs. His support of McKinley's campaign in 1896 led to his appointment as secretary of the navy in 1897.

At first Long seemed disinterested in building the fleet, but as war with Spain became more likely he became more aggressive. Once war broke out in April 1898, he took an active role and conducted the affairs of the Navy Department with vigor and competence. He was convinced from the beginning that the activities of the navy would be paramount, and he took advantage of the fifty million dollar bill to increase the size of the fleet. He worried constantly about the apparent incompetence of some of his colleagues, especially Secretary of War Russell Alger.

Long did his best to coordinate the efforts of the army and the navy during the war, but he knew that in reality joint operations were not likely because of intensive interservice rivalry. At a meeting in July 1898, Secretary of War Alger berated both Long and Admiral Mahan, claiming that lack of cooperation was their fault. Mahan responded that Alger did not know what he was talking about, and the Secretary backed down. Later, he apologized to Long for his outburst.

The controversy continued and after the Battle of Santiago a dispute arose between the army and navy over who should take possession of the Spanish ships remaining in the harbor. Possession was awarded to the navy, but tempers flared again when General Shafter refused to allow Admiral Sampson to sign the Articles of Capitulation. Long believed the struggle over the ships and the capitulation stemmed from the army's disgruntlement with the two great naval victories; the army's victory at Santiago was less dramatic and in any case owed much to naval support. Until the very end of the war Long did what he could to minimize interservice tensions, but this was a difficult and inherently impossible task because no institutional means existed within the constitutional structure of the United States government to manage joint operations.

In the Pacific Long's two major problems were the safety of Dewey's fleet after the Battle of Manila Bay and U.S. relations with Aguinaldo. There was fear that Spain might send another fleet to trap Dewey. This did not happen. Following McKinley's instructions, Long ordered Dewey to make no commitments and to enter into no real or apparent alliances. Dewey complied.

Once hostilities ended Long was among those who at first favored flexibility in dealing with Spain but in the end did not oppose the expansionist policy that emerged. Moreover, unlike many of his colleagues, he emerged from the wartime experience comparatively unscathed. Other agencies fell prey to investigations, but the Navy Department was spared because of Long's competent leadership. Long remained in the cabinet after McKinley's reelection but resigned in May 1902 after serving Theodore Roosevelt only four months. He resumed his law practice in Boston and remained there until his death on August 28, 1915.

Alfred Thayer Mahan, 1840–1914

The famous naval officer and historian was born at West Point, New York, on September 27, 1840. His father, Dennis Hart Mahan, was a professor of engineering at the U.S. Military Academy. Mahan attended a private school in Hagerstown, Maryland, studied for two more years at Columbia University, and then entered the U.S. Naval Academy. At the time he was only 16 years of age, but he was granted a commission because of his brilliance. He graduated second in his class in 1859.

At the outbreak of the Civil War Mahan held the rank of lieutenant. He saw action on the *Pocahontas* at Port Royal, spent considerable time on blockade duty, taught at the naval academy, and served on the staff of Admiral Dalhgren in 1864–1865. By the end of the war he held the rank of lieutenant commander.

Over the next 30 years Mahan spent much time at sea and eventually held several commands, but he hated the sea and was a very poor sailor. On several occasions during his long career his lack of confidence and downright incompetence caused collisions or near collisions with other vessels. Why he was never brought before a board of inquiry and why he was continually placed in command positions is not clear.

In 1885 Mahan was invited to lecture on tactics and naval history at the War College in Newport. He did such a remarkable job that in 1886 he was named president of the college, a position he held until 1889. The following year the lectures were published in book form under the title *The Influence of Sea Power upon History, 1660–1783.* This publication made Mahan famous and marked the beginning of his career as an author, commentator, and authority on naval affairs. This book traces the rise and decline of the great maritime nations, describes how a nation becomes a great sea power, and treats in much detail the relationship between naval and political history.

During the period between 1890 and 1892 Mahan researched and wrote another book, *The Influence of Sea Power upon the French Revolution and Empire, 1793–1812* (two volumes, 1892). This work also contributed to his fame. Because of such success he concluded that his true calling was writing, not seamanship. For some reason the navy disagreed, and in 1893 he was given command of the *Chicago,* flagship of the European Squadron. From the beginning of the assignment he was under enormous stress. He lived in constant fear of an accident whenever he was near other vessels, and he suffered from chronic stomach irritation. Finally, on May 27, 1893, his fears were realized when the *Chicago* brushed the USS *Bancroft,* a naval academy training ship, in the

New York Naval Shipyard. Shortly after this incident Mahan injured his knee and was placed on the restricted duty list. He never went to sea again.

Mahan retired from active duty in 1896 but was recalled to serve on the Naval War Board in May 1898. This group was organized by Secretary of the Navy Long to serve as an advisory body. Through most of the war its members included Mahan; Captain Arent S. Crowninshield, chief of the Bureau of Navigation; and Rear Admiral Montgomery Sicard, who had formerly commanded the North Atlantic Squadron. Although the board rendered important service, Mahan later minimized its significance, arguing that major decisions should always be made by one person. Nevertheless, throughout the conflict he was never reluctant to express his views. He was especially critical of Sampson's thrust toward Puerto Rico before the discovery of Cervera's whereabouts and ridiculed Miles's plans for the invasion of Puerto Rico, arguing that the Spanish garrison at San Juan could more easily be forced into surrender by naval bombardment. On the other hand, despite his low opinion of the importance of the board, he later declared that its only major error had been the delay in sending assistance to Dewey.

More important, however, was the expression of his views in his writings. Through his numerous magazine articles and his influence on people such as Theodore Roosevelt and Henry Cabot Lodge, he was a major force in stimulating American expansionist policy during that critical period between the summer of 1898 and the election of 1900. Mahan devoted himself almost exclusively to his writing during the last decade and a half of his life. He produced six major books on naval affairs in addition to several volumes of essays. He was working on a study of American expansion in relation to sea power when he died suddenly of heart failure on December 1, 1914.

José Martí, 1853–1895

Martí, the father of Cuban independence and one of the greatest Latin American men of letters, was born in Havana on January 28, 1853. He spent his early years in Spain, where he received the equivalent of a high school education, and then returned to Cuba with his family as a teenager. Soon the Ten Years' War began (1868) and Martí became involved by working for an anticolonialist newspaper. At the age of 16 he was arrested by Spanish authorities, convicted of insurrection, and sentenced to six years at hard labor.

After serving three years of his sentence Martí was exiled to Spain, where he was able to continue his education. He attended the University of Madrid and the University of Zaragosza and received degrees in law, philosophy, and letters. After graduation he moved to Mexico City, where he worked as a journalist, but his opposition to the abusive practices of the government soon forced him to leave.

At the end of the Ten Years' War the Spanish government declared a general amnesty in Cuba, and Martí returned home. He found that there had been no reforms, and his open criticism of the government resulted in another banishment to Spain. After a short time there he fled to the United States, where he lived in New York for a year before moving to Venezuela. There he worked for a short time teaching literature, but yet another dictatorial government forced him out. He returned to the United States in 1881 and, except for occasional trips abroad, resided there until his death in 1895.

While living in the United States Martí devoted himself to his writing and to his tireless advocacy of Cuban independence. In 1892 he founded the Cuban Revolutionary party and began publication of *La Patria*, a newspaper devoted to Cuban freedom. By the end of 1894 Martí was pushing for immediate revolutionary activity. His letters to Máximo Gómez and Antonio Maceo at that time reflect both his rage at the Spanish government and his fear that imperialist forces in the United States might succeed in taking over Cuba before independence could be won. Martí hated the United States almost as much as he hated Spain. He once wrote, "I have lived within the monster and know its entrails."

On March 25, 1895, Martí issued the Manifesto de Montecristo, which triggered the revolution. This proclamation called for the war to be waged by whites and blacks alike and declared that the support of all Cubans was crucial to victory and that revolution would bring new life to Cuba. In May, Martí joined Gómez in Cuba, intending to lead the revolution in person, but on the nineteenth, in one of the first skirmishes with Spanish forces, called the Battle of Dos Ríos, he was shot and killed. His comrades attempted to recover his body but were unable to do so. He was buried by Spanish authorities in Havana. Martí was gone, but his spirit lived on through his writings and propelled the revolution forward. He wrote, "Men of action, above all those whose actions are guided by love, live forever. Other famous men, those of much talk and few deeds, soon evaporate."

In 1898, the United States entered the war and seized control of affairs from the Cuban rebels. When the war ended Cuba was free but came under the domination of the United States through the Platt Amendment, a domination that lasted for three decades. Thus both Martí's greatest goal and his greatest fear were realized. Cuba was independent but at the same time controlled by "the monster of the north."

William McKinley, 1843–1901

The 25th president of the United States was born at Niles, Ohio, on January 29, 1843, the seventh of nine children. He was educated in the public schools of Poland, Ohio, and later attended Allegheny College in Pennsylvania. At the age of 17 he enlisted as a private in the Union Army and served throughout the Civil War with the Twenty-third Ohio Volunteers under Rutherford B. Hayes. He was mustered out with the brevet rank of major.

After the war McKinley opened a law office in Canton, Ohio, and soon became active in Republican Party politics. He was elected to Congress in 1876 and served continuously until 1890 with the exception of one term (1882–1884). During that time he became an expert on the tariff, which became his major issue. He favored protection and made many friends in the business world. Among them was Marcus Alonzo Hanna, a Cleveland industrialist, who backed and promoted McKinley's career throughout the 1890s. From 1888 until he left Congress McKinley was chairman of the House Ways and Means Committee, and the tariff act of 1890 bore his name.

After leaving Congress McKinley served two terms as governor of Ohio and was named the Republican candidate for president in 1896. By that time the nation was mired in the depths of a serious depression and the money question had replaced the tariff as the issue of the day. There was disagreement within the major parties, but in general the Republicans favored "sound money" as represented by the gold standard. McKinley was no expert on the subject of currency and issued only carefully scripted statements on the matter. His campaign was well funded and skillfully conducted and he comfortably defeated his Democratic opponent, William Jennings Bryan.

By March 1897 public attention was turning toward the war in Cuba, and there was growing sentiment for American intervention. McKinley was not keen on the idea at first—he had seen enough of war 35 years earlier—but swept along by public opinion and the demands of other politicians, he led America into a conflict with Spain in 1898. The war began simply as an effort to free Cuba from Spanish domination but soon developed into a struggle for the acquisition of colonies. Although Congress had disavowed any intention to annex Cuba, victory whetted an appetite for expansion, and—after considerable hesitation—McKinley approved the seizure of the Philippine Islands as well as Puerto Rico and Guam. Some politicians and businessmen—known in those days as the anti-imperialists—opposed the seizure of overseas territories, fearing such moves would lead to dangerous international entanglements, but their objections were swept aside. A peace treaty with Spain confirming American demands was ratified in 1900. In the meantime McKinley's reelection was interpreted as a public mandate for expansion.

President McKinley was only beginning to develop a policy for the administration of America's overseas possessions when he was assassinated by Leon Czolgosz, a self-proclaimed anarchist, in September 1901. He was succeeded by Theodore Roosevelt, long an all-out advocate of expansion, who would lead America into the new century with very strong policies both at home and abroad.

Wesley Merritt, 1834–1910

Wesley Merritt was born on June 16, 1834, into a family of 11 children. After an unsuccessful law career, his father moved the family to a farm in St. Clair County, Illinois, where the elder Merritt was a farmer, state legislator, and newspaper editor. Raised in the comfortable environment of an affluent and politically active household, Wesley attended the military academy at West Point, graduating in the class of 1860 and ranking 22d out of 41. Earlier, he had considered the idea of going into law, but upon graduation he joined the Second United States Dragoons. He served on the frontier and during the Civil War with distinction.

After the Civil War Merritt served in the West as lieutenant colonel of the Ninth United States Cavalry, helping to put down several Indian uprisings. In 1876 he was colonel of the Fifth U.S. Cavalry, then was commissioned a brigadier general, regular army, in 1887. He served as superintendent of West Point from 1882 until 1887, and from 1895 until 1897 took over command of the departments of the Missouri, Dakota, and East, respectively. When war broke out with Spain, Merritt commanded the U.S. forces in the Philippine Islands, cooperating with Admiral Dewey in the U.S. expedition to conquer Manila. He was the officer who accepted the Spanish surrender. Merritt served as the first military governor of the Philippines (July 25, 1898, until August 22, 1898) and then as adviser in Paris for the U.S. peace commissioners. Merritt then assumed command of the Department of the East until his retirement on June 16, 1900, after having served 40 years in the regular army. He died at Natural Bridge, Virginia, on December 3, 1910, and was buried in the cemetery at his beloved West Point.

Nelson Appleton Miles, 1839–1925

One of the great American warriors of the nineteenth century, Miles was born on August 8, 1839, on his father's farm near Westminster, Massachusetts. He received a rudimentary education and never attended college.

When the Civil War erupted Miles organized a company of a hundred volunteers who became a part of the Twenty-second Massachusetts Volunteer Regiment. He was commissioned as captain but was not allowed to command because he was considered too young. However, he soon demonstrated such extraordinary bravery and natural ability that he quickly rose through the ranks. Between 1861 and 1865 he participated in almost every major engagement of the Army of the Potomac and was wounded four times. For distinguished gallantry at Chancellorsville (May 2–4, 1863) he was awarded the Congressional Medal of Honor, and by the end of the war he held the rank of brigadier general of volunteers. He was then only 26 years of age.

After the Civil War Miles joined the regular army with the rank of colonel. During the next 15 years, while serving as commander of the Fifth Infantry, he participated in numerous engagements against hostile Indians west of the Mississippi. His exploits included victories over the

Cheyennes, Kiowas, and Comanches on the South Plains; the Sioux in the North; and the Nez Perce in the mountain west. In the late 80s he undertook successful operations against the Chiricahua Apaches led by Geronimo, and in 1890 he participated in the last official engagement of the Indian wars, the so-called Battle of Wounded Knee. By that time he held the rank of major general.

Miles became commander-in-chief of the army in 1895 and still held that position when war broke out between the United States and Spain in 1898. From the outset he worried about the timing of a large-scale invasion of Cuba, fearing that it might be attempted during the rainy season and wondering whether the navy could clear the gulf and the Caribbean of the enemy. Eventually, he proposed that a small force of regulars be sent to Cuba after the seaways were cleared, arguing that this strategy would compel the Spaniards to surrender with minimal American losses. He also hoped to take advantage of possible cooperation with the insurgents.

When it became clear that Cervera's fleet had reached Santiago, Miles altered his thinking. He now believed that it would be best to launch a simultaneous land and sea attack at Santiago, eliminate Cervera, and then take Puerto Rico as soon as possible in order to establish a base of operations against a possible future Spanish threat from the sea. Thus, in early June, he ordered General Shafter to proceed from Tampa to southern Cuba. After Santiago and Puerto Rico were captured, Miles believed it would be possible to attack Havana, but because the president and Secretary of War Alger disagreed, this plan was never initiated. McKinley wanted to concentrate on Santiago and then invade Puerto Rico, hoping to force Spain to capitulate without the need for an assault on Havana.

After operations began in Cuba Miles himself proceeded there but did not take over command from Shafter. However, he worked closely with his colleague during the 10 days between his arrival and the surrender of Spanish forces on July 17, and soon thereafter he left Cuba with his own forces to invade Puerto Rico. Miles landed at Guánica on July 25. There were several skirmishes but no major action by the time hostilities ended. Soon after that Miles and his men were evacuated.

After the war Miles was promoted to the rank of lieutenant general. He did not participate in the military operations during the insurrection in the Philippines, but he conducted an official investigation of the action and issued a report accusing the American military of atrocities. This report caused considerable controversy. He retired from active duty on August 8, 1903.

Miles was the author of several books. While still on active duty he wrote an autobiography in 1896 and a study of military affairs in Europe in 1898. His second autobiography, *Serving the Republic,* was published in 1911. During his retirement years he resided in Washington, D.C., where he died in 1925. He was buried in Arlington National Cemetery.

Patricio Montojo y Pasaron, 1839–1917

Montojo entered the Spanish navy in 1852 at the age of 13, rose through the ranks, and eventually became rear admiral. It was his misfortune to be in command of Spanish naval forces in the Philippines at the time of the Spanish-American War. His fleet consisted of 37 vessels, but only seven were capable of action, and of these none could compete with Dewey's forces. Montojo was in an impossible situation. He could not fight Dewey in Subig Bay because shore defenses there were inadequate. He could not meet Dewey at Corregidor for the same reason, and he could not disperse his forces among the islands because that would leave Manila undefended. He decided to anchor off Cavite and defend from there, knowing full well there was no chance of success.

During the Battle of Manila Bay on May 1, 1898, Montojo was wounded while directing fire from his flagship, the *Reina Maria Cristina.* When he realized that half his crew was dead or wounded he ordered the ship abandoned and scuttled to avoid further casualties. The battle was brief and ended in total disaster for the Spaniards.

Montojo retired to Spain in October 1898 and was court-martialed because he had lost his squadron. During the trial he defended himself ably but was convicted and retired from service. Subsequently, he devoted himself for the most part to his love of literature. He translated James Fenimore Cooper's novel *The Two Admirals* into Spanish and wrote essays and articles both technical and literary. One of his works was a discussion of his defeat at Manila Bay, "El desastre de Cavite, sus causes y sus efectors," which appeared in the magazine *La España Moderna* in 1909. Montojo died in 1917.

Theodore Roosevelt, 1858–1919

Born on October 27, 1858, Theodore was one of four children of Theodore and Martha Roosevelt, well-to-do residents of New York City. As a child he suffered from asthma and poor eyesight but received excellent care from his parents and, determined to overcome his difficulties, taught himself to ride, shoot, and box. He also developed an intense interest in natural history and the outdoors and became a lifelong advocate of what he called "the strenuous life."

Educated by tutors as a child, he later went to Harvard, where he was an excellent student and made Phi Beta Kappa. His senior thesis, "The Naval War of 1812," was later published and can still be found in any good library. It was the first of an outpouring of historical and literary works written by Roosevelt throughout his life. While a student at Harvard Roosevelt met, wooed, and married the beautiful Alice Lee. Shortly after graduation he decided to enter politics and ran for the state assembly from the 21st district. He won and subsequently served three terms in Albany, where he became known as a moderate reformer. This first phase of his political career was marred and ended by tragedy. On February 22, 1884, Alice died from complications of childbirth only a few hours after the death of Roosevelt's mother. Roosevelt was heartbroken and resolved to leave New York, saying, "The light has gone out of my life."

The senior Roosevelt had died in 1878, leaving Theodore more than $50,000, a princely sum in those days. He invested most of his fortune in a North Dakota cattle ranch and traveled west to oversee his holdings. Eventually, he lost most of his investment but never lost his enthusiasm for the west and the adventures it offered. From 1885 to 1889 Roosevelt also wrote six books.

Returning to politics in 1886, Roosevelt ran for mayor of New York. It was an election he could not possibly win, but the effort ingratiated him with the Republican machine. Shortly after his defeat he married Edith Carow, his childhood sweetheart, and after a honeymoon in Europe he returned to his writing. In 1888 Roosevelt supported Benjamin Harrison in his quest for the presidency and was rewarded with an appointment to the new civil service commission. For six years thereafter the Roosevelts lived in Washington and Theodore did his best to make the civil service system effective. When the reformer

William J. Strong was elected mayor of New York in 1894, Roosevelt accepted an invitation to return home to become president of the board of police commissioners. The mission of this body was to clean up the hopelessly corrupt New York City police force; Roosevelt gave it his all, although he accomplished little.

William McKinley was elected president in 1896, and, largely influenced by Roosevelt's friend Henry Cabot Lodge, he appointed Roosevelt assistant secretary of the navy. It was now early 1897—the crisis in Cuba was intensifying almost daily, and Roosevelt was among the expansionists who thought a war with Spain could bring great rewards to the United States, which was now an emerging world power. On February 25, 1898, Roosevelt, without authorization, ordered Commodore George Dewey, commander of the Asiatic Squadron, to proceed to Hong Kong and prepare to attack the Spanish fleet in the Philippines if war should break out. Secretary of the Navy John D. Long was upset by Roosevelt's action but did not rescind the order. When the war began late in April, Dewey was ready.

Roosevelt resigned his government post on May 6, 1898; requested and was given a commission; and along with his friend Colonel Leonard Wood organized a volunteer cavalry regiment that eventually gained fame as the Rough Riders, a nickname derived from the fact that many of the volunteers had participated in Buffalo Bill Cody's Wild West Show as "The Rough Riders of the West." This small force trained at San Antonio and Tampa and fought with distinction in Cuba during July 1898. Of course, Roosevelt's men were not the only heroes of the war, but their action was publicized by the journalist Richard Harding Davis and by Roosevelt himself, and the result was that they received more credit than they deserved. More importantly, Roosevelt emerged as a national hero.

Roosevelt's fame led to his successful run for governor of New York in 1898, when he was elected by a slim majority over the Democratic candidate, Augustus Van Wyck. As governor he worried the leaders of the Republican state machine, especially Senator Thomas C. Platt, not because he was liberal but because he was too independent. The party's leaders saw him as a maverick and wanted to get rid of him.

McKinley's popular vice president, Garrett Hobart, had died in 1897, leaving the second-highest office in the land vacant. In those days most politicians considered the vice presidency a dead-end job, even though it was a high honor, and Platt sought to rid himself of Roosevelt by persuading him to run for the office in 1900. After some hesitation Roosevelt accepted and was elected. McKinley was assassinated in September 1901, and suddenly Roosevelt found himself in the White House, much to the disgust of Platt and other conservative Republican leaders.

Thus by sheer chance Theodore Roosevelt became chief of state at the very time the nation and its leaders wrestled with the problems generated by the empire Roosevelt had helped to create. As president his policies in the Far East and the Caribbean were aggressive as he sought to take advantage of new conditions. His greatest achievement in that area was the building of the Panama Canal. He also achieved an impressive record on the domestic scene for his efforts to regulate big business and conserve natural resources. He died in his sleep at his home in Oyster Bay, New York, on January 6, 1919.

Práxedes Mateo Sagasta, 1825–1903

Born in 1825 in Torrecilla, Spain, of middle-class parents, Sagasta was educated as an engineer. He entered politics as a progressive, but confronted by repression, he became a revolutionary. He was forced into exile, where he continued his plotting and published a revolutionary journal. Eventually he was able to return and reenter politics under a new regime. He was prime minister in 1875 when Antonio Cánovas del Castillo and Martínez de Campos overthrew the government and placed Alfonso XII on the throne. Sagasta decided to accept the new Bourbon monarchy and, along with his followers, founded the new Liberal Party. From that time until 1899 Sagasta and Cánovas, leader of the Conservative Party, alternated as prime minister. Cánovas died in office in 1897, and María Cristina, the queen regent, called upon Sagasta to form a new government. Thus he became prime minister as the crisis with the Americans approached.

When the Cuban revolt broke out in 1895 Sagasta favored the use of force to suppress it, but by 1897 he had concluded that the best course was reform and autonomy. He did not favor independence for Cuba or any other part of the empire, believing that Spanish public opinion would never accept such a change. Because Sagasta believed that war with the United States could only lead to disaster, he sought to resolve the crisis over Cuba through diplomacy. He soon discovered, however, that such a course was nearly impossible because too few concessions would not satisfy the Americans and too many might topple the monarchy. Therefore, he reluctantly signed Spain's declaration of war on April 21, 1898.

The disastrous defeat at Manila Bay on May 1 caused a crisis in the Spanish government and prompted Sagasta to offer to resign—an offer that the queen regent rejected. By mid-July Sagasta, convinced that a negotiated settlement was his only option, agreed to an armistice that was signed on August 12. He then appointed peace commissioners, whose work led to the Treaty of Paris signed on December 10.

Inevitably, Sagasta was blamed for the defeat, but he defended himself by saying his government had done everything possible to avoid war short of submitting to humiliation. By fighting, he insisted, Spain had avoided dishonor and saved the monarchy. This was undoubtedly true, but Sagasta's government fell anyway and was replaced by a conservative regime in March 1899. Sagasta returned to power briefly in 1901–1902, but died in 1903. Upon his death the Liberal Party collapsed.

William Thomas Sampson, 1840–1902

Sampson commanded the Atlantic fleet during the Spanish-American War. He performed admirably but was never given the credit he deserved because of the unusual events associated with the Battle of Santiago.

The eldest of seven children, Sampson was born in Palmyra, New York, on February 9, 1840. An excellent student, he was appointed to the U.S. Naval Academy and graduated first in his class in 1861. Throughout most of the Civil War he served as an instructor at Annapolis, but in 1864 he was named executive officer of the monitor *Patapsco*. He was one of the few to survive when the ship was blown up in Charleston harbor on January 15, 1865.

After the war Sampson served two tours in the Atlantic and then returned to the naval academy where he was head of the physics department from 1874 to 1878. During this period he became renowned for his expertise in the fields of physics, chemistry, metallurgy, and astronomy. He was also regarded as a master teacher whose lectures were notable for their great clarity and painstaking attention to detail.

Upon leaving Annapolis in 1879 he served for three years as commanding officer of the *Swatara* in the Pacific. Following that he was stationed at the Naval Observatory and in 1884 served as a delegate to the International Meridian Conference. He then was assigned command of the Newport Torpedo Station and at the same time became a member of the interservice board on coastal defense. Following his tour as superintendent of the naval academy [1886–1890] he commanded the *San Francisco* for two years and then became superintendent of the Naval Gun Foundry in Washington. He served as chief of the Ordinance Bureau from 1893 to 1897. Sampson joined the North Atlantic Squadron in June 1897, as captain of the battleship *Iowa*. He was president of the board of inquiry on the *Maine* disaster and then was chosen to command the North Atlantic Squadron on the eve of the war with Spain. He was given this command because of his distinguished service record, even though other capable officers were more senior.

Early in the war Sampson established a blockade of the northern coast of Cuba. In May he steamed eastward to bombard San Juan, Puerto Rico, but when it became clear that Cervera's fleet had arrived in the Caribbean he returned to Cuba and linked up with the Flying Squadron under the command of Winfield Scott Schley. Together they blockaded the southern coast of Cuba, trapping Cervera in the harbor at Santiago. Sampson was in overall command of this operation and was under enormous pressure. He was responsible not only for the blockade, but also for cooperation with the army, detection of mine operations, and control over a fleet which totaled nearly 100 vessels. His health undoubtedly suffered from the stress.

On the morning of July 3, Sampson turned his ship, the *New York*, eastward intending to go ashore for a conference with General Shafter. He did not turn command over to Schley. At about 9:30 A.M. Cervera's ships began to emerge from the harbor and were immediately fired upon by the American vessels acting under Schley's orders. Sampson reversed his course and moved back toward the battle although he never became engaged. Schley, meanwhile, was in the thick of the action and when it was over the press gave him credit for the victory. Thus, Sampson's first message—"The fleet under my command offers the nation a Fourth of July present, the Whole of Cervera's fleet," was met with scorn from the public. In the eyes of the people Schley always remained the hero of the Battle of Santiago, even though the Navy Department and most high ranking officers supported Sampson. The controversy between the two men raged on for years, and, in fact, was never fully resolved.

Although Sampson planned to take his fleet to Spain itself, after the Spanish forces in the Caribbean were subdued this proved unnecessary because the war ended in mid-August. Instead, Sampson came home to the Port of New York, arriving on August 20. From September to December 1898, he was back in Cuba with the Puerto Rico Evacuation Commission; he then returned to command the North Atlantic Squadron, where he remained until October 1899. He was subsequently put in charge of the Boston Navy Yard and served there until his death on May 6, 1902.

Winfield Scott Schley, 1839–1909

Schley played a major role in the naval battle of Santiago and thus was a key figure in the outcome of the war. Born on October 9, 1839, in Frederick County, Maryland, he received his secondary education in the town of Frederick and was appointed to the U.S. Naval Academy in 1856. Shortly graduating in 1860 he went on active duty and served with distinction in the Civil War.

After the war he served in both the Atlantic and the Pacific and had two teaching assignments at the naval academy. In 1884 he led a dangerous expedition into the Arctic to rescue the survivors of a party led by Lieutenant A. W. Greely trying to reach the North Pole. He brought seven members of the expedition home safely and gained considerable recognition for this achievement. His reputation was enhanced further by the Valparaiso Affair in 1891 when two sailors from his ship, the *Baltimore*, were murdered by a Chilean mob. His firm but tactful handling of the crisis helped to avert further violence. Between 1891 and 1898 he served one tour as commander of the *New York*, and then became head of the Lighthouse Board. He was promoted to the rank of Commodore in early 1898.

At the beginning of the war Schley was selected to command the Flying Squadron operating out of Hampton Roads, Virginia. In doing so he agreed that should his squadron undertake operations in the Caribbean, he would be under the command of William T. Sampson, commander of the Atlantic Squadron, even though Sampson was slightly his junior in rank. This agreement later helped to produce the great controversy between Sampson and Schley.

When it became reasonably clear that Cervera was headed for the West Indies, probably Cuba, Schley, under Sampson's orders, established a blockade at Cienfuegos, the chief port of southern Cuba. But once it was discovered that Cervera had entered the harbor at Santiago, Schley was ordered to proceed there. He delayed, and once having arrived he reported to the Navy Department that he needed to return to Key West for coal. He was later criticized for this action because the president wanted him to stay on station. It seemed that he wavered under the responsibilities of high command even though he was an excellent officer with a distinguished record.

Schley was further criticized for his actions during the Battle of Santiago on July 3. There were two issues. First, questions arose regarding his maneuvers that nearly caused a collision between his flagship, the *Brooklyn*, and the *Texas*. Second, Sampson aboard the flagship *New York* had moved away from the harbor entrance that morning intending to go ashore for a conference with General Shafter. When Cervera emerged from the harbor Sampson swiftly reversed course and was never out of sight of the action. Nevertheless, Schley assumed that he was in command. When the battle was over and the Spanish squadron destroyed, Schley took credit and was hailed as a hero by the press and the public. Sampson protested, and eventually the matter was referred to a three-man naval court of inquiry chaired by Admiral Dewey. By a 2–1 vote Schley was mildly censored, although Dewey was sympathetic to his claims.

Because Schley was genial and approachable and Sampson was cold and aloof, public opinion always tended to favor Schley, who remained popular. He retired from the navy in October 1907 and made his home in Washington, D.C. While on a visit to New York City he died suddenly on October 2, 1909. He was buried in Arlington National Cemetery.

William R. Shafter, 1835–1906

The man who late in life would command American forces in Cuba during the Spanish-American War was born in Kalamazoo County, Michigan, on October 16, 1835. He received the equivalent of an elementary and secondary education and never attended college. In 1861 he volunteered for service in the Civil War and was commissioned a lieutenant in the Seventh Michigan Infantry. He fought in several major engagements, including the Peninsular Campaign, the Battle of Fair Oaks, and the Battle of Nashville, and on March 13, 1865, he was breveted brigadier general of volunteers. Many years later he was awarded the Congressional Medal of Honor for gallantry at Fair Oaks.

After the war he remained in the army and was assigned to frontier duty with the rank of lieutenant colonel. He rose to colonel in 1879, brigadier general in 1897, and major general in 1898. Because he had gained a reputation over the years for aggressiveness and for his ability to deal with difficult situations, he was chosen to lead the Cuban Expeditionary Force. His forces received minimal training at Tampa, Florida and sailed for Cuba on June 14, 1898. After landing at Daiquirí on June 22, Shafter and his men were engaged in combat for 10 days, at the end of which time they laid siege to the city of Santiago. On July 3, Shafter demanded the surrender of the city, but the Spanish commander, General José Velazquez Toral, initially refused. Meanwhile, the Spanish fleet in the harbor, commanded by Admiral Pascual Cervera, was destroyed, and Toral was forced to rethink his position. Under Spanish law he was not permitted to surrender as long as food and ammunition remained, but his situation was so desperate that his government granted him permission to surrender to Shafter, which he did on July 17.

Meanwhile, American forces were decimated by dysentery, malaria, and yellow fever. Shafter himself became so ill that he was confined to his tent during much of the action. Finally, the evacuation of his forces began on August 8. Of the 25,000 men who survived combat and had been in Cuba for only two months, some 80 percent were sick. Because of their condition General Shafter was harshly criticized by the press, but he actually deserved little of the blame. The nation had gone to war in the tropics unprepared and utterly ignorant of the devastating potential of tropical diseases.

Later in 1898 Shafter was assigned command of the Department of California. He remained in San Francisco until his retirement in October 1899, and then moved to a ranch near Bakersfield, where he lived with his daughter until his sudden death on November 12, 1906. He was buried at the Presido of San Francisco. In 1919 a large bust honoring him was unveiled in his hometown of Galesburg, Michigan.

Charles Dwight Sigsbee, 1845–1923

Sigsbee was born in Albany, New York, on January 16, 1845. He received his early education there and entered the U.S. Naval Academy in 1859. He graduated in 1863 and at once began his active service. During the period from 1863 to 1865 he participated in two major Civil War engagements, the Battle of Mobile Bay on August 5, 1864, and the assault on Fort Fisher in late December 1864 and early January 1865.

After the war Sigsbee served in both the Atlantic and Pacific squadrons and spent some time as an instructor at the naval academy. He also served in the Hydrographic Office; ships under his command discovered the Sigsbee Deep, the deepest part of the Gulf of Mexico, in 1878. In March 1897 he was promoted to captain and given command of the USS *Maine,* which President McKinley decided to send to Havana in early 1898 as a signal to Spain that the United States was deeply concerned about conditions in Cuba. Sigsbee and his ship arrived on January 25 and spent three uneventful weeks anchored in the harbor. Then on February 15, 1898, without warning, the *Maine* exploded, killing 266 members of the crew. The blast occurred at 9:45 P.M. while Sigsbee was in his cabin writing a letter to his wife. His first thought was to save the vessel, but he soon discovered that this was impossible and ordered the survivors to abandon ship. The *Maine* sank quickly in 50 feet of water.

Eventually, two courts of inquiry studied the disaster. The Americans concluded that the explosion was no fault of the crew and that all necessary safety precautions had been observed. They also concluded that the cause of the disaster was external, brought about by a mine situated beneath the ship. The Spaniards, on the other hand, concluded that the source of the explosion was internal, probably caused by spontaneous combustion in a coal bunker. Sigsbee believed the cause was a mine, and he never deviated from that belief. The controversy has never been fully resolved. The "yellow press" led by the *New York World* and the *New York Journal* blamed the Spaniards and most Americans agreed, although some suspected that the Cuban insurgents might have been involved. Spain had no reason to destroy an American vessel, an act almost certain to bring the United States into the war, while the insurgents very much wanted American intervention. In any case, the event, combined with pressure created by other developments, caused Spain and America to declare war on each other in April 1898.

During the war Sigsbee commanded the *St. Paul,* an auxiliary cruiser. He participated in the blockade of Cuba and the Battle of Santiago and also successfully engaged two Spanish vessels, a destroyer and a cruiser, off San Juan, Puerto Rico. Unfortunately, Sigsbee's career was damaged by his failure, while on blockade duty off Santiago, to notice the clearly visible Spanish cruiser *Cristóbal Colón* sitting in the entrance to the harbor. This oversight delayed American realization of the presence of Admiral Cervera's fleet by nearly 10 days. Because he lost the *Maine* and because of other mistakes such as this, Sigsbee was never again given command of a battleship.

After the Spanish-American War Sigsbee remained on active duty for nine years. He served as chief intelligence officer of the navy from 1900 to 1903 and after being promoted to rear admiral in 1903 was given command of the League Island Navy Yard at Philadelphia. He served in command positions in the Atlantic from 1904 to 1906, and during that period he led a special squadron detailed to carry the remains of John Paul Jones from France to the naval academy at Annapolis. Sigsbee retired in January 1907. He died in 1923.

Valeriano Weyler y Nicolau, 1838–1930

Although he had a long and, for the most part, distinguished career in the military service of Spain, Weyler is best known to history as the "butcher of Cuba" for his so-called reconcentration policies carried out in a failed effort to put down the Cuban Rebellion of 1895.

Weyler was born in Palma de Mallorca in 1838 and received his education there and in Granada. He emulated his father by joining the army and soon demonstrated great dedication and skill. At the age of 20 he was in Cuba fighting in the revolution known as the Ten Years' War and had already earned the rank of lieutenant. Returning to Spain in 1873, Weyler fought against the royalist faction known as the Carlists, who were attempting to overthrow the parliamentary government. He advanced quickly through the ranks and was promoted to general in 1878 at the age of 40. Subsequently, he was named captain general of the Canary Islands; captain general of the Philippines; and, in February 1896, governor general of Cuba. His task was to put down the rebellion that erupted in 1895.

Realizing that he faced an enemy using guerrilla tactics, Weyler sought to neutralize their effectiveness by forcing large numbers of people to enter "restricted areas" in those parts of the country where the guerrillas were most active. These restricted areas were actually concentration camps in which living conditions were appalling. Thousands died and the plan failed. To make matters worse, the American media reported conditions in Cuba in grisly detail, referring to Weyler as "the butcher." These reports in turn inflamed American public opinion and helped bring on the war. When the Liberal government came to power under Sagasta in 1897, Weyler was recalled, but the damage already done to U.S.-Spanish relations was irreparable. However, Weyler's military career was not destroyed. Upon his return to Spain he was mobbed by supporters and urged to join a conspiracy to overthrow the Liberal government. Wisely, he refused, fearing that such an effort would precipitate a civil war.

Weyler, who sincerely believed that Spain could win the war with America, blamed the politicians for the defeat. He defended the army after the war and also wrote a book defending his reconcentration policies. After the collapse of the Liberal Party Weyler served several terms as minister of war and ended his career as commander-in-chief of the army (1921–1923). He died at the advanced age of 92 in 1930.

Stewart Lyndon Woodford, 1835–1913

Woodford was born in New York City on September 3, 1835. He graduated from Columbia in 1854, studied law, and was admitted to the bar in 1857. His career was dedicated to the law, the military, politics, and public service. During the Civil War he served as a lieutenant colonel in the 127th New York Volunteers and colonel of the 103d U.S. Colonial Infantry. He was brevetted brigadier general on May 12, 1865, and retired from the military in August.

A Republican, Woodford served as a delegate to the Republican National Conventions of 1860 and 1872; as assistant U.S. attorney in New York City, 1861 and 1862; as lieutenant governor of New York from 1867 to 1869; in Congress from 1873 to 1874, and as U.S. attorney for the Southern District of New York from 1877 to 1883.

President McKinley appointed Woodford U.S. Envoy Extraordinary and Minister Plenipotentiary to Spain on June 19, 1897. From the date of his arrival in Madrid until war was declared in April 1898, he attempted to preserve peace between the United States and Spain. In so doing he exhibited a disturbingly naive approach to international diplomacy. Shortly after his arrival Spanish authorities made clear to Woodford their belief that the Cuban insurrection continued only because of U.S. support. Woodford countered with a threat that the United States expected Spain to bring about an armistice by November, or else the United States would take "any necessary steps." At this point Práxedes Mateo Sagasta came to power as prime minister. He favored peace and promised Woodford that Cuba would be offered autonomy. Nevertheless, Woodford remained pessimistic, believing that Sagasta had come to power too late. However, his attitude changed late in October when he was informed that Cuba would be given autonomy in January 1898.

Unfortunately, autonomy did not work in Cuba because neither the rebels nor the pro-Spanish elements wanted it. The rebels believed they could still achieve independence whereas the pro-Spanish felt their best interests would be served by maintaining their colonial status. Woodford persuaded himself that some form of compromise could be reached that would prevent war, but with the revelation of the Dupuy de Lôme letter and the destruction of the *Maine* in February, circumstances changed. President McKinley, now under great pressure to intervene, sent Woodford an ultimatum to be presented to the Spanish government. It demanded that the concentration camps be closed, that an armistice be declared, and that Spain recognize Cuba's independence. Woodford violated his instructions in delivering this message. He omitted the demand that Spain grant Cuba independence. It is not clear why he did so, but he probably assumed there was still some chance for a negotiated settlement. In this belief he demonstrated the naïveté of an inexperienced diplomat in that he never understood that for Spain the loss of Cuba was unthinkable; it would undoubtedly bring about the fall of the dynasty. Even those Spanish leaders who wanted peace would opt for war before they would allow the monarchy to fall.

Despite Woodford's' efforts, war was declared between the United States and Spain in April 1898. He resigned his post and returned to the United States, where he resumed the practice of law. He died in New York City on February 14, 1913.

Primary Documents of the Spanish-American War

Document 1
The Dupuy de Lôme Letter

In December 1897, Señor Don Dupuy de Lôme wrote this letter to his friend Señor Don José Canalejas. Canalejas was a respected Spanish journalist and Prime Minister Sagasta's informal representative in Cuba. The letter contains some unflattering remarks about President McKinley. It was stolen in Cuba—exactly how is not known—and delivered to the Cuban junta in New York City. The junta offered it to the media, and the first newspaper to publish it was William Randolph Hearst's *New York Herald* on February 9, 1898. It created an immediate sensation and generated demands that Dupuy de Lôme resign, which he did. The impact of the letter on public opinion combined with that generated by the *Maine* disaster a week later helped propel the nation toward war.

His Excellency Don José Canalejas,

My distinguished and dear Friend: You have no reason to ask my excuses for not having written to me. I ought also to have written to you, but I have put off doing so because overwhelmed with work . . .

The situation here remains the same. Everything depends on the political and military outcome in Cuba. The prologue of all this, in this second stage (phase) of the war, will end the day when the colonial cabinet shall be appointed and we shall be relieved in the eyes of this country of a part of the responsibility for what is happening in Cuba, while the Cubans, whom these people think so immaculate, will have to assume it.

Until then, nothing can be clearly seen, and I regard it as a waste of time and progress, by a wrong road, to be sending emissaries to the rebel camp, or to negotiate with the autonomists who have as yet no legal standing, or to try to ascertain the intentions and plans of this Government. The [Cuban] refugees will keep on returning one by one, and as they do so will make their way into the sheepfold, while the leaders in the field will gradually come back. Neither the one nor the other class had the courage to leave in a body and they will not be brave enough to return in a body.

The message has been a disillusionment to the insurgents, who expected something different; but I regard it as bad (for us).

Besides the ingrained and inevitable bluntness (grosería) with which is repeated all that the press and public opinion in Spain have said about Weyler, it once more shows what McKinley is, weak and a bidder for the admiration of the crowd, besides being a would-be politician (politicastro) who tries to leave a door open behind himself while keeping on good terms with the jingoes of his party.

Nevertheless, whether the practical results of it [the message] are to be injurious and adverse depends upon ourselves.

I am entirely of your opinions; without a military end of the matter nothing will be accomplished in Cuba, and without a military and political settlement there will always be the danger of encouragement being given to the insurgents by a part of the public opinion if not by the Government.

I do not think sufficient attention has been paid to the part England is playing.

Nearly all the newspaper rabble that swarms in your hotels are Englishmen, and while writing for the *Journal* they are also correspondents of the most influential journals and reviews of London. It has been so ever since this thing began. As I look at it, England's only object is that the Americans should amuse themselves with us and leave her alone, and if there should be a war, that would the better stave off the conflict which she dreads but which will never come about.

It would be very advantageous to take up, even if only for effect, the question of commercial relations, and to have a man of some prominence sent hither in order that I may make use of him here to carry on a propaganda among the Senators and others in opposition to the junta and to try to win over the refugees . . . .

Ever your attached friend and servant.

Enrique Dupuy De Lôme.

Source: *Papers Relating to the Foreign Relations of the United States,* December 5, 1898 (Washington: U.S. Government Printing Office, 1901), pp. 1007–8.

Document 2
Senator Redfield Proctor's Speech

On March 17, 1898, Senator Redfield Proctor (R-Vermont) delivered a powerful speech on the floor of the U.S. Senate. In it he described what he had seen on a recent trip to Cuba. Before the trip he had not believed that conditions in Cuba could be as horrific as the media reported. He discovered that the reality was actually worse. Proctor's speech persuaded many people who had previously been hesitant that war with Spain was necessary for humanitarian reasons to save the Cuban people from the barbaric abuses of the Spaniards. Although there was no persuasive evidence to support this view, many people also believed that Senator Proctor spoke for President McKinley, and this made his words even more influential. Following are excerpts from the speech.

Mr. PROCTOR: Mr. President, more importance seems to be attached by others to my recent visit to Cuba than I have given it, and it has been suggested that I make a public statement of what I saw and how the situation impressed me. This I do on account of the public interest in all that concerns Cuba, and to correct some inaccuracies that have, not unnaturally, appeared in reported interviews with me.

My trip was entirely unofficial and of my own motion, not suggested by anyone. The only mention I made of it to the President was to say to him that I contemplated such a trip, and to ask him if there was any objection to it; to which he replied that he could see none. No one but myself, therefore, is responsible for anything in this statement. Judge Day gave me a brief note of introduction to General Lee [Fitzhugh Lee, the U.S. Consul-General in Havana], and I had letters of introduction from business friends at the North to bankers and other business men at Habana, and they in turn gave me letters to their correspondents in other cities. These letters to business men were very useful, as one of the principal purposes of my visit was to ascertain the views of practical men of affairs upon the situation . . .

The *Maine*

It has been stated that I said there was no doubt the *Maine* was blown up from the outside. This is a mistake. I may have said that such was the general impression among Americans in Havana. In fact, I have no opinion about it myself, and carefully avoided forming one. I gave no attention to these outside surmises. I met the members of the court on their boat, but would as soon approach our Supreme Court in regard to a pending cause as that board. They are as competent and trustworthy within the lines of their duty as any court in the land, and their report, when made, will carry conviction to all the people that the exact truth has been stated just as far as it is possible to ascertain it. Until then surmise and conjecture are idle and unprofitable. Let us calmly wait for the report.

The Reconcentrados—The Country People

All the country people in the four western provinces, about 400,000 in number, remaining outside the fortified towns when Weyler's order was made were driven into these towns, and these are the "reconcentrados." They were the peasantry, many of them farmers, some landowners, others renting lands, and owning more or less stock, others working on estates and cultivating small patches; and even a small patch in that fruitful clime will support a family.

It is but fair to say that the normal condition of these people was very different from what prevails in this country. Their standard of comfort and prosperity was not high measured by ours. But according to their standards and requirements their conditions of life were satisfactory.

They lived mostly in cabins made of palms or in wooden houses. Some of them had houses of stone, the blackened walls of which are all that remain to show the country was ever inhabited.

The first clause of Weyler's order read as follows:

I ORDER AND COMMAND

First, All the inhabitants of the country or outside of the line of fortifications of the towns shall, within the period of eight days, concentrate themselves in the towns occupied by the troops. Any individual who, after the expiration of this period, is found in the uninhabited parts will be considered a rebel and tried as such.

The other three sections forbid the transportation of provisions from one town to another without permission of the military authority, direct the owners of cattle to bring them into the towns, prescribed that the eight days shall be counted from the publication of the proclamation in the head town of the municipal district, and state that if news is furnished of the enemy which can be made use of, it will serve as a "recommendation."

Many, doubtless did not learn of this order. Others failed to grasp its terrible meaning. Its execution was left largely to the guerrillas to drive in all that had not obeyed, and I was informed that in many cases the torch was applied to their homes with no notice, and the inmates fled with such clothing as they might have on, their stock and other belongings being appropriated by the guerrillas. When they reached the towns, they were allowed to build huts of palm leaves in the suburbs and vacant places within the trochas, and left to live, if they could.

Their huts are about 10 by 15 feet in size, and for want of space are usually crowded together very closely. They have no floor but the ground, no furniture and after a year's wear, but little clothing except such stray substitutes as they can extemporize; and with large families or more than one, in this little space, the commonest sanitary provisions are impossible. Conditions are unmentionable in this respect. Torn from their homes, with foul earth, foul air, foul water, and foul food or none, what wonder that one-half have died and that one-quarter of the living are so diseased that they can not be saved? A form of dropsy is a common disorder resulting from these conditions. Little children are still walking about with arms and chest terribly emaciated, eyes swollen, and abdomen bloated to three times the natural size. The physicians say these cases are hopeless.

Deaths in the streets have not been uncommon. I was told by one of our consuls that they have been found dead about the markets in the morning, where they had crawled, hoping to get some stray bits of food from the early hucksters, and that there had been cases where they had dropped dead inside the market surrounded by food. Before Weyler's order, these people were independent and self-supporting. They are not beggars even now. There are plenty of professional beggars in every town among the regular residents, but these country people, the reconcentrados, have not learned the art. Rarely is a hand held out to you for alms when going among their huts, but the sight of them makes an appeal stronger than words.

The Spaniard

I had little time to study the race question, and have read nothing on it, so can only give hasty impressions. It is said that there are nearly

200,000 Spaniards in Cuba out of a total population of 1,600,000. They live principally in the towns and cities. The small shopkeepers in the towns and their clerks are mostly Spaniards. Much of the larger businesses, too, and of the property in the cities, and in a less degree in the country, is in their hands. They have an eye to thrift, and as everything possible in the way of trade and legalized monopolies, in which the country abounds, is given to them by the Government, many of them acquire property. I did not learn that the Spanish residents of the island had contributed largely in blood or treasure to suppress the insurrection.

The Cuban

There are, or were before the war, about 1,000,000 Cubans on the island. 200,000 Spaniards (which means those born in Spain), and less than half a million of negroes and mixed bloods. The Cuban whites are of pure Spanish blood and, like the Spaniards, dark in complexion, but oftener light or blond, so far as I noticed. The percentage of colored to white has been steadily diminishing for more than fifty years, and is not now over 25 per cent of the total. In fact the number of colored people has been actually diminishing for nearly that time. The Cuban farmer and laborer is by nature peaceable, kindly, gay, hospitable, light-hearted, and improvident.

There is a proverb among the Cubans that "Spanish bulls can not be bred in Cuba,"—that is, the Cubans, though they are of Spanish blood, are less excitable and of a quieter temperament. Many Cubans whom I met spoke in strong terms against the bull fights; that it was a brutal institution, introduced and mainly patronized by the Spaniards. One thing that was new to me was to learn the superiority of the well-to-do Cuban over the Spaniard in the matter of education. Among those in good circumstances there can by no doubt that the Cuban is far superior in this respect. And, the reason of it is easy to see. They have been educated in England, France, or this country, while the Spaniard has such education as his own country furnishes.

The Military Situation

It is said that there are about 60,000 Spanish soldiers now in Cuba fit for duty out of the more than 200,000 that have been sent there. The rest have died, have been sent home sick, or in hospitals, and some have been killed, notwithstanding the official reports. They are conscripts, many of them very young, and generally small men. One hundred and thirty pounds is a fair estimate of their average weight. They are quiet and obedient, if well-drilled and led, I believe would fight fairly well, but not at all equal to our men. Much more would depend on the leadership than with us. The officer must lead well and be one in whom they have confidence, and this applies to both sides alike. As I saw no drills or regular formation, I inquired about them of many persons, and was informed that they had never seen a drill. I saw perhaps 10,000 Spanish troops, but not a piece of artillery or a tent. They live in barracks in the towns, and are seldom out for more than the day, returning to town at night.

They have little or no equipment for supply trains or for a field campaign such as we have. Their cavalry horses are scrubby little native ponies, weighing not over 800 pounds, tough and hardy, but for the most part in wretched condition, reminding one of the mount of Don Quixote. Some of the officers, however, have good horses, mostly American, I think. On both sides cavalry is considered the favorite and the dangerous fighting arm. The tactics of the Spanish, as described to me by eyewitnesses and participants in some of their battles, is for the infantry, when threatened by insurgent cavalry, to form a hollow square and fire away. . . . without ceasing until time to march back to town.

It does not seem to have entered the minds of either side that a good infantry force can take care of itself and repulse anywhere an equal or greater number of cavalry, and there are everywhere positions where cavalry would be at a disadvantage.

Having called on Governor and Captain-General Blanco and received his courteous call in return, I could not with propriety seek communication with insurgents. I had plenty of offers of safe conduct to Goméz's camp, and was told that if I would write him, an answer would be returned safely within ten days at most.

I saw several who had visited the insurgent camps, and was sought out by an insurgent field officer, who gave me the best information received as to the insurgent force. His statements were moderate, and I was credibly informed that he was entirely reliable. He claimed that the Cubans had about 30,000 men now in the field, some in every province, but mostly in the two eastern provinces, and eastern Santa Clara, and this statement was corroborated from other good sources.

They have a force all the time in Havana province itself, organized in four small brigades and operating in small bands. Ruiz was taken, tried, and shot within about a mile and a half of the railroad and about 15 miles out of Havana, on the road to Matanzas, a road more traveled than any other, and which I went over four times.

Arranguren was killed about 3 miles the other side of the road and about the same distance, 15 or 20 miles, from Havana. The Cubans are well armed, but very poorly supplied with ammunition. They are not allowed to carry many cartridges; sometimes not more than one or two. The infantry, especially, are poorly clad. Two small squads of prisoners which I saw, however, one of half a dozen in the streets of Havana, and one of three, wore better clothes than the average Spanish soldier.

Each of these prisoners, though surrounded by guards, was bound by the arm and wrists by cords, and they were all tied together by a cord running along the line, a specimen of the amenities of their warfare. About one-third of the Cuban army are colored, mostly in the infantry, as the cavalry furnished their own horses.

This field officer, an American from a Southern State, spoke in the highest terms of the conduct of these colored soldiers; that they were as good fighters and had more endurance than the whites; could keep up with the cavalry on a long march and come in fresh at night.

The Political Situation

The dividing lines between parties are the straightest and clearest cut that have ever come to my knowledge. Two divisions in our war were by no means so clearly defined. It is Cuban against Spaniard. It is practically the entire Cuban population on one side and the Spanish army and Spanish citizen on the other.

I do not count the autonomists in this division, as they are so far too inconsiderable in numbers to be worth counting. General Blanco filled the civil offices with men who had been autonomists and were still classed as such. But the march of events had satisfied most of them that the chance for autonomy came too late.

It falls as talk of compromise would have fallen the last year or two of our war. If it succeeds, it can only be by armed force, by the triumph of the Spanish army, and the success of Spanish arms would be easier by Weyler's policy and method, for in that the Spanish army and people believe.

There is no doubt that General Blanco is acting in entire good faith; that he desires to give the Cubans a fair measure of autonomy, as Campos did at the close of the ten-year war. He has, of course, a few personal followers, but the army and the Spanish citizens do not want genuine autonomy for that means government by the Cuban people. And it is not strange that the Cubans say it comes too late.

I have never had any communication, direct or indirect, with the Cuban Junta in this country or any of its members, nor did I have with any of the juntas which exists in every city and large town of Cuba. None of the calls I made were upon parties of whose sympathies I had the least knowledge, except that I knew some of them were classed as autonomists.

Most of my informants were business men, who had taken no sides and rarely expressed themselves. I had no means of guessing in advance what their answers would be, and was in most cases greatly surprised at their frankness. I inquired in regard to autonomy of men of wealth and men as prominent in business as any in the cities of Habana, Matanzas, and Sagua, bankers, merchants, lawyers, and autonomist officials, some of them Spanish born but Cuban bred, one prominent Englishman, several of them known as autonomists, and several of them telling me they were still believers in autonomy if practicable, but without exception they replied that it was "too late" for that.

Some favored a United States protectorate, some annexation, some free Cuba; not one has been counted favoring the insurrection at first. They were business men and wanted peace, but said it was too late for peace under Spanish sovereignty. They characterized Weyler's order in far stronger terms than I can. I could not but conclude that you do not have to scratch an autonomist very deep to find a Cuban. There is soon to be an election, but every polling place must be inside a fortified town. Such elections ought to be safe for the "ins".

I have endeavored to state in not intemperate mood what I saw and heard, and to make no argument thereon, but leave everyone to draw his own conclusions. To me the strongest appeal is not the barbarity practiced by Weyler nor the loss of the *Maine*, if our worst fears should prove true, terrible as are both of these incidents, but the spectacle of a million and a half of people, the entire native population of Cuba, struggling for freedom and deliverance from the worst misgovernment of which I ever had knowledge. But whether our action ought to be influenced by any one or all these things, and, if so, how far, is another question.

I am not in favor of annexation: not because I would apprehend any particular trouble from it, but because it is not wise policy to take in any people of foreign tongue and training, and without any strong guiding American element. The fear that if free the people of Cuba would be revolutionary is not so well founded as has been supposed, and the conditions for good self-government are far more favorable. The large number of educated and patriotic men, the great sacrifices they have endured, the peaceable temperament of the people, whites and blacks, the wonderful prosperity that would surely come with peace and good home rule, the large influx of American and English immigration and money, would all be strong factors for stable institutions.

But it is not my purpose at this time, nor do I consider it my province, to suggest any plan. I merely speak of the symptoms as I saw them, but do not undertake to prescribe. Such remedial steps as may be required may safely be left to an American President and the American people.

Source: *Congressional Record—Senate,* March 17, 1898, pp. 2916–19.

Document 3
The Spanish Declaration of War

The Sagasta government did everything possible to prevent the crisis from reaching a flash point in hopes that by some miracle war could be avoided. By the time the Cortes opened formal debate on the issue on April 20, however, it appeared that all options had been exhausted. Spain's course was guided by two imperatives: the queen regent's determination to preserve the monarchy for her son, and the Liberal members' determination to preserve constitutional government. It was feared that both would be toppled if the government failed to fight and defend Spain's honor. Having received an ultimatum from the United States that could not be fully accepted, on April 23, 1898, the Spanish crown declared war against the United States.

By agreement of my Cabinet, in the name of my royal son, the King Alfonso XIII, as Regent Queen of the Kingdom, I decree:

1st : War status existing between Spain and United States compels us to cancel the Treaty of Peace and Friendship of October 27, 1795, the Protocol of January 12, 1877 and all agreements, pacts and conventions that, until today, exist between both countries.

2nd : From the proclamation of this Royal Decree, all American ships anchored in Spanish harbors can leave with freedom during the following five days.

3rd : Although Spain has not signed the agreement of Paris, dated April 16, 1857, because Spain has declared his purpose for not adhering to that agreement, my Government, in consideration of international law, wants to observe and orders to observe the following rules of maritime law:

A) Neutral flags protect the enemy trade goods, except contraband of war.

B) Neutral trade goods, except contraband of war, can not be confiscated when under the enemy flag.

C) Blockades, for being obligatories, may be effectives, held by a capable force to prevent the arrival at enemy coasts.

4th : Holding up our right to give letters of marque for Privateers, that was reserved by note of May 16, 1857, when Spanish Government answered to French Government about the Spanish attachment to the Maritime Law's agreement of Paris, Spanish Government shall fit out, with Spanish Merchant Ships, a service of Auxiliary Cruisers that co-operate with the navy during the war and under its command.

5th : With a purpose to capture enemy ships, to confiscate enemy trade goods under its own flag and to confiscate contraband of war under any flag, the right of inspection on high seas or enemy waters can be exercised by the Royal Navy, Auxiliary cruisers and privateers, when these are used, according to international Law.

6th : Guns, machine-guns, howitzers, rifles and any fire arms or side arms; bombs, grenades, bullets, fuses, wicks, powder, sulphur, dynamite and all explosives; equipment such as uniforms, cartridge boxes, saddle-horses, harness for artillery and cavalry; engines for ships, screw propellers, boilers and other goods which can be used for building, refitting or equipping warships or, in general, any instruments, items, or goods that can be used for war are considered as Contraband of War.

7th : Captains, skippers, officers of ships, or when two third parts of crew, not being Americans make acts of war against Spain, will be considered as pirates and they will be judged with all law severity although they are protected by American letters of marque for privateers.

8th : State and Navy Ministers are entrusted to execute this Royal Decree and they can command the necessary orders to best carry it out.

Signed in the Royal Palace on April 23, 1898.
Regent Queen Maria Cristina

Source: The Spanish-American War Centennial Web site (http://www.spanam.simplenet.com/declarationwarspain.htm)

Document 4
The United States Declaration of War

On April 11, 1898, President McKinley asked Congress for authority to intervene in Cuba after receiving an unsatisfactory response to the ultimatum of March 27. On April 19, Congress responded with a joint resolution authorizing intervention. Two days later Spain broke diplomatic relations, and on April 23 declared war on the United States. McKinley went before Congress on April 25 asking for a declaration of war on Spain; Congress obliged later the same day. However, the American declaration of war was made retroactive to April 21, the day on which Spain broke diplomatic relations.

Executive Mansion, Washington April 25, 1898.
To the Senate and House of Representatives of the United States of America:

I transmit to the Congress for its consideration and appropriate action, copies of correspondence recently had with the representative of Spain in the United States, with the United States minister at Madrid, and through the latter with the Government of Spain, showing the action taken under the joint resolution approved April 20, 1898, "for the recognition of the independence of the people of Cuba, demanding that the Government of Spain relinquish its authority and Government in the island of Cuba, and to withdraw its land and naval forces from Cuba and

Cuban waters, and directing the President of the United States to use the land and naval forces of the United States to carry these resolutions into effect."

Upon communicating to the Spanish minister in Washington the demand which it became the duty of the Executive to address to the Government of Spain in obedience, to said resolution, the minister asked for his passports and withdrew. The United States minister at Madrid was in turn notified by the Spanish minister for foreign affairs that the withdrawal of the Spanish representative from the United States had terminated diplomatic relations between the two countries, and that all official communications between their respective representatives ceased therewith.

I commend to your especial attention the note addressed to the United States minister at Madrid by, the Spanish minister of foreign affairs on the 21st instant, whereby the foregoing notification was conveyed. It will be perceived therefrom that the Government of Spain, having cognizance of the joint resolution of the United States Congress, and in view of the things which the President is thereby required and authorized to do, responds by treating the reasonable demands of this Government as measures of hostility, following with that instant and complete severance of relations by its action which by the usage of nations accompanies an existent state of war between sovereign powers.

The position of Spain being thus made known, and the demands of the United States being denied, with a complete rupture of intercourse, by the act of Spain, I have been constrained, in the exercise of the power conferred upon me by the joint resolution aforesaid, to proclaim, under date of April 22, 1898, a blockade of certain ports of the north coast of Cuba, between Cardenas and Bahia Honda, and the port of Cienfugos, on the south coast of Cuba, and to issue my proclamation dated April 23, 1898, calling forth volunteers.

I now recommend the adoption of a joint resolution declaring that a state of war exists between the United States of America and the Kingdom of Spain, that the definition of the international status of the United States as a belligerent power may be made known and the assertion of all its rights in the conduct of a public war may be assured.

WILLIAM McKINLEY.

DECLARATION OF WAR WITH SPAIN

Be it enacted by the Senate and House of Representatives of the United States of America in Congress assembled, First. That war be, and the same is hereby, declared to exist, and that war has existed since the 21st day of April, A.D. 1898, including said day, between the United States of America and the Kingdom of Spain.

Second. That the President of the United States be, and he hereby is, directed and empowered to use the entire land and naval forces of the United States and to call into the actual service of the United States the militia of the several States to such extent as may be necessary to carry this act into effect.

Approved, April 25 1898.

Source: *Presidential Messages and State Papers,* vol. 8 (New York: Review of Reviews Company, 1917), pp. 2967–69.

Document 5
The Teller Amendment

During the Senate debate on the president's request for authority to intervene in Cuba, Senator Henry Moore Teller, Silver Republican of Colorado, introduced an amendment disclaiming any intent by the United States to annex Cuba. Teller favored expansion but opposed securing Cuba by force. He believed that after the Spaniards were driven out the time would soon come when the Cubans would be clamoring for annexation. Although there was heated debate in the Senate over the resolution to intervene, Teller's proposal was accepted with virtually no opposition.

Whereas the abhorrent conditions which have existed for more than three years in the Island of Cuba, so near our own borders, have shocked the moral sense of the people of the United States, have been a disgrace to Christian civilization, culminating, as they have, in the destruction of a United States battle ship, with two hundred and sixty-six of its officers and crew, while on a friendly visit in the harbor of Havana, and cannot longer be endured, as has been set forth by the President of the United States in his message to Congress of April eleventh, eighteen hundred and ninety-eight, upon which the action of Congress was invited: Therefore,

Resolved, First. That the people of the Island of Cuba are, of right ought to be, free and independent.

Second. That it is the duty of the United States to demand, and the Government of the United States does hereby demand, that the Government of Spain at once relinquish its authority and government in the Island of Cuba and withdraw its land and naval forces from Cuba and Cuban waters.

Third. That the President of the United States be, and he hereby is, directed and empowered to use the entire land and naval forces of the United States, and to call into the actual service of the United States the militia of the several States, to such extent as may be necessary to carry these resolutions into effect.

Fourth. That the United States hereby disclaims any disposition or intention to exercise sovereignty, jurisdiction, or control over said Island except for the pacification thereof, and asserts its determination, when that is accomplished, to leave the government and control of the Island to its people.

Source: *The World of 1898: The Spanish-American War,* Hispanic Division, Library of Congress.

Document 6
Theodore Roosevelt's Description of the Attack on Kettle Hill

In this description of the attack on Kettle Hill (July 1, 1898), Theodore Roosevelt emphasizes only the movements of his own unit, although several others were involved. He also exaggerates slightly in asserting that he gave the order to charge. The order was actually given by Lieutenant John D. Miley, General Shafter's aide. Roosevelt also minimizes the horrors of the assault. It was made without adequate artillery support and was very costly. The Americans suffered over 1,000 casualties.

This event was very important in the life of Theodore Roosevelt because it catapulted him to fame, made him a national hero, and led to his election as governor of New York and vice president of the United States. In September 1901, the assassination of McKinley sent him to the White House.

Meanwhile we of the left wing had by degrees become involved in a fight which toward the end became not even a colonel's fight, but a squad leader's fight. The cavalry division was put at the head of the line. We were told to march forward, cross a little river in front, and then, turning to the right, march up alongside the stream until we connected with Lawton. Incidentally, this movement would not have brought us into touch with Lawton in any event. But we speedily had to abandon any thought of carrying it out. The maneuver brought us within fair range of the Spanish entrenchments along the line of hills which we called the San Juan Hills, because on one of them was the San Juan blockhouse. On that day my regiment had the lead of the second brigade, and we marched down the trail following in trace behind the first brigade. Apparently the Spaniards could not make up their minds what to do as the three regular regiments of the first brigade crossed and defiled along the other bank of the stream, but when our regiment was crossing they began to fire at us.

Under this flank fire it soon became impossible to continue the march. The first brigade halted, deployed, and finally began to fire back. Then our brigade was halted. From time to time some of our men would fall, and I sent repeated word to the rear to try to get authority to attack the hills in front. Finally, General Sumner, who was fighting the division in fine shape, sent word to advance. The word was brought to me by Mills, who said that my orders were to support the regulars in the assault on the hills, and that my objective would be the red-tiled ranch-house in front, on a hill which we afterwards christened Kettle Hill. I mention Mills saying this because it was exactly the kind of definite order the giving of which does so much to insure success in a fight, as it prevents all obscurity as to what is to be done. The order to attack did not reach the first brigade until after we ourselves reached it, so that at first there was doubt on the part of their officers whether they were at liberty to join in the advance.

I had not enjoyed the Guasimas fight at all, because I had been so uncertain as to what I ought to do. But the San Juan fight was entirely different. Spaniards had a hard position to attack, it is true, but we could see them, and I knew exactly how to proceed. I kept on horseback, merely because I found it difficult to convey orders along the line, as the men were lying down; and it is always hard to get men to start when they cannot see whether their comrades are also going. So I rode up and down the lines, keeping them straightened out, and gradually worked through line after line until I found myself at the head of the regiment. By the time I had reached the lines of the regulars of the first brigade I had come to the conclusion that it was silly to stay in the valley firing at the hills, because that was really where we were most exposed, and that the thing to do was to try to rush the entrenchments. Where I struck the regulars there was no one of superior rank to mine, and after asking why they did not charge, and being answered that they had no orders, I said I would give the order. There was naturally a little reluctance shown by the elderly officer in command to accept my order, so I said, "Then let my men through, sir," and I marched through, followed by my grinning men. The younger officers and the enlisted men of the regulars jumped up and joined us. I waved my hat, and we went up the hill with a rush. Having taken it, we looked across at the Spaniards in the trenches under the San Juan blockhouse to our left, which Hawkins's brigade was assaulting. I ordered our men to open fire on the Spaniards in the trenches.

Memory plays funny tricks in such a fight, where things happen quickly, and all kinds of mental images succeed one another in a detached kind of way, while the work goes on. As I gave the order in question there slipped through my mind Mahan's account of Nelson's orders that each ship as it sailed forward, if it saw another ship engaged with an enemy's ship, should rake the latter as it passed. When Hawkins's soldiers captured the blockhouse, I, very much elated, ordered a charge on my own hook to a line of hills still farther on. Hardly anybody heard this order, however; only four men stayed with me, three of whom were shot. I gave one of them, who was only wounded, my canteen of water, and ran back, much irritated that I had not been followed—which was quite unjustifiable, because I found that nobody had heard my orders. General Sumner had come up by this time, and I asked his permission to lead the charge. He ordered me to do so, and this time away we went, and stormed the Spanish entrenchments. There was some close fighting, and we took a few prisoners. We also captured the Spanish provisions, and ate them that night with great relish. One of the items was salted flying-fish, by the way. There were also bottles of wine, and jugs of fiery spirit, and as soon as possible I had these broken, although not before one or two of my men had taken too much liquor. Lieutenant Howze, of the regulars, an aide of General Sumner's, brought me an order to halt where I was; he could not make up his mind to return until he had spent an hour or two with us under fire. The Spaniards attempted a counter-attack in the middle of the afternoon, but were driven back without effort, our men laughing and cheering as they rose to fire; because hitherto they had been assaulting breastworks, or lying still under artillery fire, and they were glad to get a chance to shoot at the Spaniards in the open. We lay on our arms that night and as we were drenched with sweat, and had no blankets save a few we took from the dead Spaniards, we found even the tropic night chilly before morning came.

During the afternoon's fighting, while I was the highest officer at our immediate part of the front, Captains Boughton and Morton of the regular cavalry, two as fine officers as any man could wish to have beside him in battle, came along the firing line to tell me that they had heard a rumor that we might fall back, and that they wished to record their emphatic protest against any such course. I did not believe there was any truth in the rumor, for the Spaniards were utterly incapable of any effective counter-attack. However, late in the evening, after the fight, General Wheeler visited us at the front, and he told me to keep myself in readiness, as at any moment it might be decided to fall back. Jack Greenway was beside me when General Wheeler was speaking. I answered, "Well, General, I really don't know whether we would obey an order to fall back. We can take that city by a rush, and if we have to move out of here at all I should be inclined to make the rush in the right direction." Greenway nodded an eager assent. The old General, after a moment's pause, expressed his hearty agreement, and said that he would see that there was no falling back. He had been very sick for a couple of days, but, sick as he was, he managed to get into the fight. He was a gamecock if ever there was one, but he was in very bad physical shape on the day of the fight. If there had been any one in high command to supervise and press the attack that afternoon, we would have gone right into Santiago. In my part of the line the advance was halted only because we received orders not to move forward, but to stay on the crest of the captured hill and hold it.

We are always told that three-o'clock-in-the-morning courage is the most desirable kind. Well, my men and the regulars of the cavalry had just that brand of courage. At about three o'clock on the morning after the first fight, shooting began on our front and there was an alarm of a Spanish advance. I was never more pleased than to see the way in which the hungry, tired, shabby men all jumped up and ran forward to the hill-crest, so as to be ready for the attack; which, however, did not come. As soon as the sun rose the Spaniards again opened upon us with artillery. A shell burst between Dave Goodrich and myself, blacking us with powder, and killing and wounding several of the men immediately behind us.

Next day the fight turned into a siege; there were some stirring incidents; but for the most part it was trench work. A fortnight later Santiago surrendered.

Source: *Theodore Roosevelt: An Autobiography* (New York: Scribners, 1920) pp. 241–44.

Document 7
Lieutenant Joaquim Bustamente's Account
of the Sinking of the *Furor*

Lieutenant Joaquim Bustamente was the executive officer of the Spanish destroyer *Furor,* the last vessel to emerge from the harbor at Santiago. Within minutes of being sighted by the Americans the *Furor* was engulfed in fire from four battleships with heavy damage and casualties, but the little ship was actually sunk by fire from the unprotected yacht *Galveston* under the command of Lieutenant Commander Richard Wainwright, who had survived the destruction of the *Maine*. The *Furor* went down at approximately 11:00 A.M. with heavy loss of life. Lieutenant Bustamente was among the few Spanish sailors who made it to shore safely.

Lt. Bustamente Reports on the *Furor*

When we got to the bay's mouth, we saw our squadron [Cervera's four cruisers had exited the bay previous to the *Furor* and *Pluton*], and decided, that if we went to west, we could gain the protection of our squadron. But there was some distance between us and [the] squadron. One shell hit on our hatch, where our boiler's ventilators were located, so our steam pressure reduced considerably, and our speed slowed. At this time we had suffered a great quantity of hits. One shell cut up the boatswain in half and the part of his body fell into the steering control line. As a result of this, the ship lost partial rudder control. We needed to clear the body from the steering control line. Next, a shell destroyed the steam governor. A third exploded on the poop deck magazine and destroyed it.

We had torpedoes cleared for action. Fuses were screwed in place, but we were unable to fire because, the distance was too great during the battle. As a result of these circumstances the commander of both destroyers, Capitan de Navio Villamil ordered us to abandon ship. Myself and part of the crew leaped overboard about three miles off the coast.

In the water I saw one of my comrades (probably the boatswain) was killed by a bullet to the head. At this time our destroyer, after a series of explosions, sank. When we got to the coast, we went on foot east toward Santiago. Shortly afterwards, we met the men of Lieutenant Caballero (senior officer of TERROR) and together proceeded to Santiago.

Source: José Muller Tejeria, *Combates y Capitulación de Santiago* (Madrid, 1898).

Document 8
New York Times Editorial, July 30, 1898
Not for Cuba Only

This editorial reflects clearly the belief shared by many that the war was fought largely for reasons of self-interest that did not necessarily have anything to do with territorial expansion. Here, as late as the end of July, the *Times* is still saying what had consistently been stated all summer: that intervention in Cuba was necessary to calm the fears of the American people and to drive the Spaniards out of the Western Hemisphere.

Let us take no more credit for noble unselfishness than is justly our due. Undoubtedly we went to war to free Cuba from the dreadful rule of the Spaniard. Our pity was awakened by the sufferings of the Cubans, our indignation was aroused by the barbarism of their rulers. It is a war of humanity.

But it is not that alone. Our primary object, the real inspiring cause and chief end sought was the attainment of peace and tranquility at home. It was the "perilous unrest" among our own people to which President McKinley referred in his message to Congress that most of all provoked us to make war as a measure of prudence and self-interest.

We could not tolerate the disturbances among our own people to which the cruelties and disorders in Cuba gave rise. It was an unrest that manifested itself in continual endeavors to fit out unlawful expeditions and in countless attempted violations of our neutrality laws, demanding of our Government large expenditures and unceasing vigilance for their repression.

Had the Island of Cuba been situated in the distant Pacific or the Indian Ocean mere pity for the distress of the tortured inhabitants would never have prompted us to go to war with Spain for their relief. Our nearness to this hell upon earth made us deeply susceptible to emotions that would have been but faintly stirred by a remoter appeal. The unrest was perilous because acute and spreading, and that was due not to the flagrancy of the crime but to the propinquity of the scene of it.

This test at once shows us that humanity was not the chief ground of intervention. Neither did we intervene in the interest of the Republic of Cuba, which we wisely declined to recognize. Sympathy with a people struggling to be free we feel and are proud to feel. Only the cankered and perverse among us delight in calling such a people brigands and in dwelling upon every fresh exhibition of the unamiable qualities with which race and long oppression have endowed them. But we did not go to war to establish the Republic of Cuba.

First of all, we went to war in our own interest, to restore peace and tranquility at home and to safeguard them against the danger of repeated interruption. That was, in fact, our only strictly legal ground of intervention, as *The Times* demonstrated before war was declared. But this was a motive of self-interest. So viewed, the war was not mainly a war of humanity, but a war to suppress an international nuisance that had become intolerable and dangerous to ourselves. Self-protection first, then humanity, and the solid satisfaction of feeling that we were the instrument of historical destiny in expelling Spain from this hemisphere.

It is well not to forget fundamental facts, not only because we ought not to let an admiring world go unwarned of its mistake when it praises us for waging a purely altruistic war, but also to shut the mouths of the carpers who loudly exclaim that a war begun for the Cubans should have been terminated by our withdrawal in disgust the moment a Cuban camp follower was caught stealing bacon.

Source: *New York Times,* July 30, 1898.

Document 9
Farewell Message of the Spanish Troops

The Spanish soldiers who defended Santiago against General Shafter and his men fought with great courage. They did not believe they had been defeated. Nevertheless, they congratulated the Americans on their victory and wished them well. This is one of the most unusual documents in the history of modern warfare.

SOLDIERS OF THE AMERICAN ARMY:

We would not be fulfilling our duty as well-born men in whose breasts there live gratitude and courtesy should we embark for our beloved Spain without sending to you our most cordial and sincere good wishes and farewell. We fought you with ardor, with all our strength, endeavoring to gain the victory, but without the slightest rancor or hate toward the American nation. We have been vanquished by you (so our generals and chiefs judged in signing the capitulation), but our surrender and the bloody battle preceding it have left in our souls no place for resentment against the men who fought us nobly and valiantly.

You fought and acted in compliance with the same call of duty as we, for we all represent the power of our respective States. You fought us as men face to face and with great courage, as before stated, a quality which we had not met with during the three years we have carried on this war against a people without religion, without morals, without conscience and of doubtful origin, who could not confront the enemy, but, bidden, shot their noble victims from ambush and then immediately fled. This was the kind of warfare we had to sustain in this unfortunate land.

You have complied exactly with all the laws and usages of war as recognized by the armies of the most civilized nations of the world; have given honorable burial to the dead of the vanquished; have cured their wounded with great humanity; have respected and cared for your prisoners and their comfort; and, lastly, to us, whose condition was terrible, you have, given freely of food, of your stock of medicines, and you have honored us with distinction and courtesy, for after the fighting the two armies mingled with the utmost harmony.

With the high sentiment of appreciation from us all, there remains but to express our farewell, and with the greatest sincerity we wish you all happiness and health in this land, which will no longer belong to our, dear Spain but will be yours, who have conquered it by force and watered it with your blood as your conscience called for, under the demand of civilization and humanity.'

From 11,000 Spanish soldiers
Pedro Lopez de Castillo, Soldier of Infantry
Santiago de Cuba, August 21, 1898.

Source: A. Holloway, *Hero Tales of the American Soldier and Sailor* (Philadelphia: Elliott, 1899), pp. 127–28.

Document 10
"Mr. Dooley" Comments on Admiral Dewey's Heroics, The Invasion of Puerto Rico, and the Philippine Campaign

Finley Peter Dunne (1867–1936) was a journalist in Chicago in the 1880s and 1890s who attracted a vast audience with his political satire. He created a fictional character, Martin J. Dooley, through whom he commented on local and national events. Beginning with his first column in 1892, Dunne had the Irish neighborhood bartender comment on practically every conceivable political, social, and economic issue. Most of Dooley's conversations took place with his favorite customer, Mr. Hennessy. Dunne produced about three hundred columns between 1892 and 1899, when Dunne left Chicago for New York, but the most famous were produced during the Spanish-American War in 1898. These were published in book form under the title *Mr. Dooley: In Peace and In War* and made Dunne a national celebrity. It was one of Theodore Roosevelt's favorite books. Three examples are reproduced here: "On Admiral Dewey's Activity," "On General Miles's Moonlight Excursion," and "On the Philippines."

In the first excerpt Mr. Dooley is commenting on Admiral George Dewey's victory at Manila Bay. He is complaining that Dewey seems to want to continue his exploits until he conquers Spain itself. This is an exaggeration, of course, because Dewey's orders were to hold his position until the arrival of reinforcements. He followed these instructions to the letter. When Mr. Dooley refers to "Mack," he is talking about General Arthur MacArthur, who led American forces to victory in the so-called Philippine Insurrection. In the second excerpt Mr. Dooley is commenting on General Nelson Miles's invasion of Puerto Rico. Miles sought glory, but his forces so overwhelmed the Spanish defenders that there was actually little fighting. In any case, the people of the island welcomed the Americans, and the war ended just 18 days after their arrival.

The third excerpt finds Mr. Dooley and Mr. Hennessy discussing the Philippine question. Mr. Hennessy is all for taking the islands, but Mr. Dooley says he cannot make up his mind. In this discussion he is mocking President McKinley's indecision.

ON ADMIRAL DEWEY'S ACTIVITY

"If they don't catch up with him pretty soon," said Mr. Dooley, "he'll fight his way ar-round th' wurruld, an' come out through Barsaloona or Cades."

"Who's that?" asked Mr. Hennessy.

"Me Cousin George, no less," said Mr. Dooley. "I suppose ye think th' war is over an' peace has rayturned jus' because Tiddy Rosenfelt is back home again an' th' sojers ar-re hungry in New York 'stead iv in Sandago. That's where ye'er wrong, Hinnissy. That's where ye'er wrong, me bucko. Th' war is not over till Cousin George stops fightin'. Th' Spanyards have had enough, but among thrue fightin' men it don't make anny diff'rence what th' feelin's iv th' la-ad undherneath may be. 'Tis whin th' man on top has had his fill iv fightin' that th' throuble's over, an' be the look iv things Cousin George has jus' begun to take tay.

"Whin me frind Mack con-cluded 'twas time f'r us to stop fightin' an' begin skinning each other in what Hogan calls th' marts iv thrade, ye thought that ended it. So did Mack. He says, says he, 'Let us have peace,' he says. An' Mark Hanna came out iv' th' cellar, where he's been since Cousin George presinted his compliments to th' Ph'lippines an' wud they prefer to be kilt or dhrownded, an' pro-posals was made to bond th' Cubian pathrites, an' all th' deuces in th' deck begun to look like face car-rds again, whin suddenly there comes a message fr'm Cousin George. 'In pursooance iv ordhers that niver come,' he says, 'to-day th' squadhron undher my command knocked th' divvle out iv th' fortifications iv th' Ph'lippines, bombarded the city, an' locked up th' insurgent gin'ral. The gov'nor got away be swim-mm' aboard a Dutch ship, an' th' Dutchman took him to Ding Dong. I'll attind to th' Dutchman some afthernoon whin I have nawthin' else to do. I'm settin' in the palace with me feet on th' pianny. Write soon. I won't get it. So no more at prisint, fr'm ye'er ol' frind an' well-wisher, George Dooley.'

"How ar-re they goin' to stop him? How ar-re they goin' to stop him? There's Mack on th' shore bawlin' ordhers. 'Come back,' he says. 'Come back, I com-mand ye,' he says. 'George, come back,' he says. 'Th' war is over,' he says. 'We're at peace with th' wurruld,' he says. 'George,' he says, 'George, be a good fellow,' he says. 'Lave up on thim,' he says. 'Hivins an' earth, he's batin' that poor Spanyard with a pavin' block. George, George, ye break me hear-rt,' he says.

"But George Dooley, he gives th' wink to his frinds, an' says he, 'What's that man yellin' on th' shore about?' he says. 'Louder,' he says. 'I can't hear ye,' he says. 'Sing it,' he says. 'Write it to me on a postal ca-ard at Mahdrid,' he says. 'Don't stop me now,' he says. 'This is me, busy day,' he says; an' away he goes with a piece iv lead pipe in wan hand an' a couplin' pin in th' other.

"What'll we do with him? We can't catch up with him. He's goin' too fast. Mack's a week behind him ivry time he stops annywhere. He has sthrung a throlley acrost th' islands, an' he's climbin' mountains with his fleet. Tb' on'y thing I see, Hinnissy, that Mack can do is to go east an' meet him comin' r-round. If he hurries, he'll sthrike him somewhere in Rooshia or Boohlgahria, an' say to him: 'George, th' war's over. Won't ye come home with me?' I think he'll listen to reason."

"I think a man ought to stop flghtin' whin th' war is ended," said Mr. Hennessy.

"I dinnaw about that," said Mr. Dooley. "He started without askjn' our lave, an' I don't see what we've got to do with th' way he finishes. 'Tis a tur-rble thing to be a man iv high sperrits, an' not to know whin th' other fellow's licked."

ON GENERAL MILES'S MOONLIGHT EXCURSION

"DEAR, oh, dear,' said Mr. Dooley, "I'd give five dollars—an' I'd kill a man *f'r* three—if I was out iv this Sixth Wa-ard tonight, an' down with Gin'ral Miles' gran' picnic an' moonlight excursion in Porther Ricky. 'Tis no comfort in bein' a cow'rd whin ye think iv thim br-rave la-ads facin' death be suffication in bokays an' dyin' iv waltzin' with th' pretty girls iv Porther Ricky.

"I dinnaw whether Gin'ral Miles picked out th' job or whether 'twas picked out f'r him. But, annyhow, whin he got to Sandago de

Cubia an' looked ar-round him, he says to his frind Gin'ral Shafter, 'Gin'ral,' says he, 'ye have done well so far,' he says. 'Tis not f'r me to take th' loris fr'm th' steamin' brow iv a thrue hero; he says. 'I lave ye here,' he says, 'f'r to complete th' victhry ye have so nobly begun,' he says. 'F'r you,' he says, 'th' wallop in th' eye fr'm th' newspaper ray-porther, th' r-round robbing, an' th' sunsthroke,' he says, 'f'r me th' hardship iv th' battlefield, th' late dinner, th' theavter party, an' th' sick-enin' polky,' he says. 'Gather,' he says, th' fruits iv ye'er bravery,' he says. 'Return,' he says, 'to ye'er native land, an' receive anny gratichood th' Sicrety iv War can spare fr'm his own fam'ly,' he says. 'F'r me,' he says, 'there is no way but *f'r* to tur-rn me back upon this festive scene,' he says, 'an' go where jooty calls me,' he says. Ordherly,' he says, 'put a bot-tle on th' ice, an' see that me goold pants that I wear with th' pale blue vest with th' di'mon buttons~s irned out,' he says. An' with a haggard face he walked aboord th' excursion steamer, an' wint away.

"I'd hate to tell ye iv th' thriles iv th' expedition, Hinnissy. Whin th' picnic got as far as Punch, on th' southern coast iv Porther Ricky, Gin'ral Miles gazes out, an' says he, 'This looks like a good place to hang th' hammicks, an' have lunch,' says he. 'Forward, brave men,' says he, 'where ye see me di'mon's sparkles' says he. 'Forward, an' plant th' crokay ar-rches iv our beloved counthry,' he says. An' in they wint, like inthrepid warryors that they ar-re. On th' beach they was met be a dili-gation *fr'm* th' town of Punch, con-sistin' iv th' mayor, th' common council, th' polis an' fire departments, th' Gr-rand Ar-rmy iv th' Ray-public, an' prominent citizens in carredges. Gin'ral Miles, makin' a hasty tielet, advanced onflinchingly to meet thim. 'Gintlemen,' says he, 'what can I do f'r ye?' he says. 'We come,' says th' chairman iv th' comity, 'f'r to offer ye,' he says, 'th' r-run iv th' town,' he says. 'We have held out,' he says, 'as long as we cud,' he says. 'But,' he says, 'they'se a limit to human endurance,' he says. 'We can withstand ye no longer,' he says. 'We surrinder. Take us prisoners, an' rayceive us into ye'er glory-ous an' well-fed raypublic,' he says. 'Br-rave men,' says Gin'ral Miles, 'I congratulate ye,' he says, 'on th' heeroism iv yer definse,' he says. 'Ye stuck manfully to yer colors, whativer they ar-re,' he says. 'I on'y wond-her that ye waited f'r me to come befure surrindhrin',' he says. 'I wel-come ye into th' Union,' he says. 'I don't know how th' Union'll feel about it, but that's no business iv mine,' he says. 'Ye will get ye'er wur-rkin-cards fr'm th' walkin' diligate,' he says; 'an' ye'll be entitled,' he says, 'to pay ye'er share iv th' taxes an' to live awhile an' die whin ye get r-ready,' he says, 'jus' th' same as if ye was bor-rn at home,' he says. 'I don't know th' names iv ye; but I'll call ye all Casey, f'r short,' he says. 'Put ye'er bokays in th' hammick,' he says, 'an' return to Punch,' he says; 'an' freeze somethin' f'r me,' he says, 'f'r me thrawt is parched with th' labors iv th' day,' he says. Th' r-rest iv th' avenin' was spint in dancin',' music, an' boat-r-ridin'; an' an inj'yable time was had.

"Th' flex' day th' army moved on Punch; an' Gin'ral Miles marched into th' ill-fated city, preceded be flower-girls sthrewin' r-roses an geranyums befure him. In th' afthernoon they was a lawn tinnis party, an' at night the gin'ral attinded a banket at th' Gran' Palace Hotel. At midnight he was serenaded be th' Raymimber th' Maine Banjo an' Mandolin Club. Th' entire popylace attinded, with pork chops in their buttonholes to show their pathreetism. Th' flex' day, afther breakfastin' with Mayor Casey, he set out on his weary march over th' r-rough, flower-strewn paths f'r San Joon. He has been in gr-reat purl fr'm a witherin' fire iv bokays, an' he has met an' overpowered some iv th' mos' savage orators in Porther Ricky; but, whin I las' heerd iv him, he had pitched his tents an' ice-cream freezers near the inimy's wall, an' was grajully silencin' thim with proclamations."

"They'll kill him with kindness if he don't look out," said Mr. Hennessy.

"I dinnaw about that," said Mr. Dooley; "but I know this, that there's th' makin' iv gr-reat statesmen in Porther Ricky. A proud people that can switch as quick as thim la-ads have nawthin' to lam in th' way iv what Hogan calls th' signs iv gover'mint, even fr'm th' Supreme Court."

ON THE PHILIPPINES

"I know what I'd do if I was Mack," said Mr. Hennessy. "I'd hist a flag over th' Ph'lippeens, an' I'd take in th' whole lot iv thim."

"An' yet," said Mr. Dooley, "'tis not more thin two months since ye larned whether they were islands or canned goods. Ye'er back yard is so small that ye'er cow can't turn r-round without buttin' th' woodshed off th' premises, an' ye wudden't go out to th' stock yards without takin' out a policy on yer life. Suppose ye was standin' at th' corner iv State Sthreet an' Archey R-road, wud ye know what car to take to get to th' Ph'lippeens? If yer son Packy was to ask ye where th' Ph'lippeens is, cud ye give him anny good idea whether they was in Rooshia or jus' west iv th' thracks?"

"Mebbe I cudden't," said Mr. Hennessy, haughtily, "but I'm f'r takin' thim in, annyhow."

"So might I be," said Mr. Dooley, "if I cud on'y get me mind on it. Wan iv the worst things about this here war is th' way it's makin' puzzles f'r our poor, tired heads. Whin I wint into it, I thought all I'd have to do was to set up here behind th' bar with a good tin-cint see-gar in me teeth, an' toss dinnymite bombs into th' hated city iv Havanna. But look at me now. Th' war is still goin' on; an' ivry night, whin I'm countin' up the cash, I'm askin' mesilf will I annex Cubia or lave it to the Cubians? Will I take Porther Ricky or put it by? An' what shud I do with the Ph'lippeens? Oh, what shud I do with thim? I can't annex thim because I don't know where they ar-re. I can't let go iv thim because some wan else'll take thim if I do. They are eight thou- san' iv thim islands, with a popylation iv wan hundherd millyon naked savages; an' me bedroom's crowded now with me an' th' bed. How can I take thim in, an' how on earth am I goin' to cover th' nakedness iv thim savages with me wan shoot iv clothes? An' yet 'twud break me heart to think iv givin' people I niver see or heerd tell iv back to other people I don't know. An', if I don't take thim, Schwartzmeister down th' sthreet, that has half me thrade already, will grab thim sure.

"It ain't that I'm afraid iv not doin' th' r-right thing in th' end, Hinnissy. Some mornin' I'll wake up an' know jus' what to do, an' that I'll do. But 'tis th' annoyance in th' mane time. I've been r-readin' about th' counthry. 'Tis over beyant ye'er left shoulder whin ye're facin' east. Jus' throw ye'er thumb back, an' ye have it as ac'rate as anny man in town. 'us farther thin Boohlgahrya an' not so far as Blewchoochoo. It's near Chiny, an' it's not so near; an', if a man was to bore a well through fr'm Goshen, Indianny, he might sthrike it, an' thin again he might not. It's a poverty-sthricken counthry, full iv goold an' precious stones, where th' people can pick dinner off th' threes an' ar-re starvin' because they have no stepladders. Th' inhabitants is mostly naygurs an' Chinnymen, peaceful, industhrus, an' law-abidin', but savage an' bloodthirsty in their methods. They wear no clothes except what they have on, an each woman has five husbands an' each man has five wives. Th' r-rest goes into th' discard, th' same as here. Th' islands has been ownded be Spain since befure th' fire; an' she's threated thim so well they're now up in ar-rms again her, except a majority iv thim which is thurly loyal. Th' natives seldom fight, but whin they get mad at wan another they r-run-a-muck. Whin a man r-runsa-muck, sometimes they hang him an' sometimes they discharge him an' hire a new motorman. Th' women ar-re beautiful, with languishin' black eyes, an' they smoke see-gars, but ar-re hurried an' incomplete in their dhress. I see a pitcher iv wan th' other day with nawthin' on her but a basket of cocoanuts an' a hoop-skirt. They're no prudes. We import juke, hemp, cigar wrappers, sugar, an' fairy tales fr'm th' Ph'lippeens, an' export six-inch shells an' th' like. Iv late th' Ph'lippeens has awaked to th' fact that they're behind th' times, an' has received much American amminitiOn in their midst. They say th' Spanyards is all tore up about it.

"I larned all this fr'm th' papers, an' I know 'tis sthraight. An' yet, Hinnissy, I dinnaw what to do about th' Ph'lippeens. An' I'm all alone in th' wurruld. Ivrybody else has made up his mind. Ye ask anny con-ducthor on Ar-rchy R-road, an' he'll tell ye. Ye can find out fr'm the papers; an', if ye really want to know, all ye have to do is to ask a prom~ nent citizen who can mow all th' lawn he owns with a safety razor. But I don't know."

"Hang on to thim," said Mr. Hennessy, stoutly. "What we've got we must~hold."

"Well," said Mr. Dooley, "if I was Mack, I'd lave it to George. I'd say: 'George,' I'd say, 'if ye're f'r hangin' on, hang on it is. If ye say, lave go, I dhrop thim.' 'Twas George won thim with th' shells, an' th' question's up to him."

Source: Finley Peter Dunne, *Mr. Dooley in Peace and War* (Champaign-Urbana: University of Illinois Press, 1898), pp. 20–29.

Document 11
The Protocol of Peace
August 12, 1898

This document was negotiated by Jules Cambon, French ambassador to the United States, who acted on behalf of Spain with full powers, and William R. Day, the American secretary of state. It was a preliminary peace agreement that left the matter of the final disposition of the Philippines to be determined later at a peace conference. Nevertheless, the terms are harsh enough that the Spanish government agreed to it with great misgivings.

THE PROTOCOL OF PEACE

Embodying the Terms of a Basis for the Establishment of Peace Between the Two Countries

August 12, 1898

William R. Day, Secretary of State of the United States, and His Excellency Jules Cambon, Ambassador Extraordinary and Plenipotentiary of the Republic of France at Washington, respectively possessing for this purpose full authority from the Governments of the United States and the Government of Spain, have concluded and signed the following articles, embodying the terms on which the two Governments have agreed in respect to the matters hereinafter set forth, having in view the establishment of peace between the two countries, that is to say:

Article I.

Spain will relinquish all claim of sovereignty over and title of Cuba.

Article II.

Spain will cede to the United States the Island of Puerto Rico and other islands now under Spanish sovereignty in the West Indies, and also an island in the Ladrones to be selected by the United States.

Article III.

The United States will occupy and hold the city, bay and harbor of Manila, pending the conclusion of a treaty of peace which shall determine the control, disposition, and government of the Philippines.

Article IV.

Spain will immediately evacuate Cuba, Puerto Rico, and other islands now under Spanish sovereignty in the West Indies; and to this end each Government will, within ten days after the signing of this protocol, appoint Commissioners, and the Commissioners so appointed shall, within 30 days after the signing of the protocol, meet at Havana for the purpose of arranging and carrying out the details of the aforesaid evacuation of Cuba and the adjacent Spanish islands; and each Government will, within ten days after the signing of this protocol, meet at San Juan, in Puerto Rico, for the purpose of arranging and carrying out the details of the aforesaid evacuation of Puerto Rico and other islands now under Spanish sovereignty in the West Indies.

Article V.

The United States and Spain will each appoint not more than five Commissioners to treaty of peace and the Commissioners so appointed shall meet in Paris no later than October 1, 1898. And proceed to the negotiation and conclusion of a treaty of peace, which treaty shall be subject to ratification according to the respective constitutional forms of the two countries.

Article VI.

Upon the conclusion and signing of this protocol, hostilities between the two countries shall be suspended, and notice to that effect shall be given as soon as possible by each Government to the commanders of its military and naval forces.

Done at Washington in duplicate, in English and in French, by the undersigned, who have hereunto set their hands and seals, the 12th day of August 1898.

(Signed) William R. Day
(Signed) Jules Cambon

Source: Charles I. Blevans, ed., *Treaties and Other International Agreements of the United States of America, 1776–1949,* vol. 11 (Washington, D.C.: U.S. Government Printing Office, 1974), pp. 613–14.

Document 12
McKinley's Instructions to the Peace Commission, September 1898

Here the president sets forth his reasons for deciding that the United States could not withdraw from the Philippines and instructs the commissioners to demand—at a minimum—cession of the Island of Luzon. He had probably already made up his mind to take the entire Philippine archipelago but was not ready to say so publicly. Finally, near the end of October he revealed his true intentions. The decision to take the Philippines was one of the most momentous ever made by an American president, for it drew the nation inevitably into the turmoil of Far East international politics.

By a protocol signed at Washington August 12, 1898 . . . it was agreed that the United States and Spain would each appoint not more than five commissioners to treat of peace, and that the commissioners so appointed should meet at Paris not later than October 1, 1898, and proceed to the negotiation and conclusion of a treaty of peace, which treaty should be subject to ratification according to the respective constitutional forms of the two countries.

For the purpose of carrying into effect this stipulation, I have appointed you as commissioners on the part of the United States to meet and confer with commissioners on the part of Spain.

As an essential preliminary to the agreement to appoint commissioners to treat of peace, this government required of that of Spain the unqualified concession of the following precise demands:

The relinquishment of all claim of sovereignty over and title to Cuba.

The cession to the United States of Puerto Rico and other islands under Spanish sovereignty in the West Indies.

The cession of an island in the Ladrones, to be selected by the United States.

The immediate evacuation by Spain of Cuba, Puerto Rico, and other Spanish islands in the West Indies.

The occupation by the United States of the city, bay, and harbor of Manila pending the conclusion of a treaty of peace which should determine the control, disposition, and government of the Philippines.

These demands were conceded by Spain, and their concession was, as you will perceive, solemnly recorded in the protocol of the 12th of August. . . .

It is my wish that throughout the negotiations entrusted to the Commission the purpose and spirit with which the United States accepted the unwelcome necessity of war should be kept constantly in view. We took up arms only in obedience to the dictates of humanity and in the fulfillment of high public and moral obligations. We had no design of aggrandizement and no ambition of conquest. Through the long course of repeated representations which preceded and aimed to avert the struggle, and in the final arbitrament of force, this country was impelled solely by the purpose of relieving grievous wrongs and removing long-existing conditions which disturbed its tranquillity, which shocked the moral sense of mankind, and which could no longer be endured.

It is my earnest wish that the United States in making peace should follow the same high rule of conduct which guided it in facing war. It should be as scrupulous and magnanimous in the concluding settlement as it was just and humane in its original action. The luster and the moral strength attaching to a cause which can be confidently rested upon the considerate judgment of the world should not under any illusion of the hour be dimmed by ulterior designs which might tempt us into excessive demands or into an adventurous departure on untried paths. It is believed that the true glory and the enduring interests of the country will most surely be served if an unselfish duty conscientiously accepted and a signal triumph honorably achieved shall be crowned by such an example of moderation, restraint, and reason in victory as best comports with the traditions and character of our enlightened republic.

Our aim in the adjustment of peace should be directed to lasting results and to the achievement of the common good under the demands of civilization, rather than to ambitious designs. The terms of the protocol were framed upon this consideration. The abandonment of the Western Hemisphere by Spain was an imperative necessity. In presenting that requirement, we only fulfilled a duty universally acknowledged. It involves no ungenerous reference to our recent foe, but simply a recognition of the plain teachings of history, to say that it was not compatible with the assurance of permanent peace on and near our own territory that the Spanish flag should remain on this side of the sea. This lesson of events and of reason left no alternative as to Cuba, Puerto Rico, and the other islands belonging to Spain in this hemisphere.

The Philippines stand upon a different basis. It is nonetheless true, however, that without any original thought of complete or even partial acquisition, the presence and success of our arms at Manila imposes upon us obligations which we cannot disregard. The march of events rules and overrules human action. Avowing unreservedly the purpose which has animated all our effort, and still solicitous to adhere to it, we cannot be unmindful that, without any desire or design on our part, the war has brought us new duties and responsibilities which we must meet and discharge as becomes a great nation on whose growth and career from the beginning the ruler of nations has plainly written the high command and pledge of civilization.

Incidental to our tenure in the Philippines is the commercial opportunity to which American statesmanship cannot be indifferent. It is just to use every legitimate means for the enlargement of American trade; but we seek no advantages in the Orient which are not common to all. Asking only the open door for ourselves, we are ready to accord the open door to others. The commercial opportunity which is naturally and inevitably associated with this new opening depends less on large territorial possession than upon an adequate commercial basis and upon broad and equal privileges. . . .

In view of what has been stated, the United States cannot accept less than the cession in full right and sovereignty of the island of Luzon. It is desirable, however, that the United States shall acquire the right of entry for vessels and merchandise belonging to citizens of the United States into such ports of the Philippines as are not ceded to the United States upon terms of equal favor with Spanish ships and merchandise, both in relation to port and customs charges and rates of trade and commerce, together with other rights of protection and trade accorded to citizens of one country within the territory of another. You are therefore instructed to demand such concession, agreeing on your part that Spain shall have similar rights as to her subjects and vessels in the ports of any territory in the Philippines ceded to the United States.

Source: *Papers Relating to Foreign Affairs, 1898* (Washington, D.C.: U.S. Government Printing Office, 1901), pp. 904–8.

Document 13
The Treaty of Peace Between the United States and Spain

By this treaty the United States formally acquired an overseas empire, taking Puerto Rico, Guam, and the Philippines from Spain. Many Americans opposed such expansion and there was considerable debate—some of it highly emotional—over the ratification of the treaty. What is often forgotten, however, is what the United States did *not* take from Spain in 1898. There was no demand that

Spain cede her island possessions in the Carolinas, the Palaus, and the Marianos (except for Guam). A little later Germany bought these islands from Spain, held them for 20 years, and then lost them to Japan in negotiations following World War I. After a stormy debate the Senate ratified the treaty on February 6, 1899.

TREATY OF PEACE BETWEEN THE UNITED STATES AND SPAIN; December 10, 1898

The United States of America and Her Majesty the Queen Regent of Spain, in the name of her august son Don Alfonso XIII, desiring to end the state of war now existing between the two countries, have for that purpose appointed as plenipotentiaries:

The President of the United States, William R. Day, Cushman K. Davis, William P. Frye, George Gray, and Whitelaw Reid, citizens of the United States;

And Her Majesty the Queen Regent of Spain,

Don Eugenio Montero Rios, president of the senate, Don Buenaventura de Abarzuza, senator of the Kingdom and ex-minister of the Crown; Don José de Garnica, deputy of the Cortes and associate justice of the supreme court; Don Wenceslao Ramirez de Villa-Urrutia, envoy extraordinary and minister plenipotentiary at Brussels, and Don Rafael Cerero, general of division;

Who, having assembled in Paris, and having exchanged their full powers, which were found to be in due and proper form, have, after discussion of the matters before them, agreed upon the following articles:

Article I.

Spain relinquishes all claim of sovereignty over and title to Cuba. And as the island is, upon its evacuation by Spain, to be occupied by the United States, the United States will, so long as such occupation shall last, assume and discharge the obligations that may under international law result from the fact of its occupation, for the protection of life and property.

Article II.

Spain cedes to the United States the island of Puerto Rico and other islands now under Spanish sovereignty in the West Indies, and the island of Guam in the Marianas or Ladrones.

Article III.

Spain cedes to the United States the archipelago known as the Philippine Islands, and comprehending the islands lying within the following line:

A line running from west to east along or near the twentieth parallel of north latitude, and through the middle of the navigable channel of Bachi, from the one hundred and eighteenth (118th) to the one hundred and twenty-seventh (127th) degree meridian of longitude east of Greenwich, thence along the one hundred and twenty seventh (127th) degree meridian of longitude east of Greenwich to the parallel of four degrees and forty five minutes (4°45′) north latitude, thence along the parallel of four degrees and forty five minutes (4°45′) north latitude to its intersection with the meridian of longitude one hundred and nineteen degrees and thirty five minutes (119°35′) east of Greenwich, thence along the meridian of longitude one hundred and nineteen degrees and thirty five minutes (119°35′) east of Greenwich to the parallel of latitude seven degrees and forty minutes (7°40′) north, thence along the parallel of latitude of seven degrees and forty minutes (7°40′) north to its intersection with the one hundred and sixteenth (116th) degree meridian of longitude east of Greenwich, thence by a direct line to the intersection of the tenth (10th) degree parallel of north latitude with the one hundred and eighteenth (118th) degree meridian of longitude east of Greenwich, and thence along the one hundred and eighteenth (118th) degree meridian of longitude east of Greenwich to the point of beginning. The United States will pay to Spain the sum of twenty million dollars ($20,000,000) within three months after the exchange of the ratifications of the present treaty.

Article IV.

The United States will, for the term of ten years from the date of the exchange of the ratifications of the present treaty, admit Spanish ships and merchandise to the ports of the Philippine Islands on the same terms as ships and merchandise of the United States.

Article V.

The United States will, upon the signature of the present treaty, send back to Spain, at its own cost, the Spanish soldiers taken as prisoners of war on the capture of Manila by the American forces. The arms of the soldiers in question shall be restored to them.

Spain will, upon the exchange of the ratifications of the present treaty, proceed to evacuate the Philippines, as well as the island of Guam, on terms similar to those agreed upon by the Commissioners appointed to arrange for the evacuation of Porto Rico and other islands in the West Indies, under the Protocol of August 12, 1898, which is to continue in force till its provisions are completely executed.

The time within which the evacuation of the Philippine Islands and Guam shall be completed shall be fixed by the two Governments. Stands of colors, uncaptured war vessels, small arms, guns of all calibre, with their carriages and accessories, powder, ammunition, livestock, and materials and supplies of all kinds, belonging to the land and naval forces of Spain in the Philippines and Guam, remain the property of Spain. Pieces of heavy ordnance, exclusive of field artillery, in the fortifications and coast defences, shall remain in their emplacements for the term of six months, to be reckoned from the exchange of ratifications of the treaty; and the United States may, in the meantime, purchase such material from Spain, if a satisfactory agreement between the two Governments on the subject shall be reached.

Article VI.

Spain will, upon the signature of the present treaty, release all prisoners of war, and all persons detained or imprisoned for political offences, in connection with the insurrections in Cuba and the Philippines and the war with the United States.

Reciprocally, the United States will release all persons made prisoners of war by the American forces, and will undertake to obtain the release of all Spanish prisoners in the hands of the insurgents in Cuba and the Philippines.

The Government of the United States will at its own cost return to Spain and the Government of Spain will at its own cost return to the United States, Cuba, Porto Rico, and the Philippines, according to the situation of their respective homes, prisoners released or caused to be released by them, respectively, under this article.

Article VII.

The United States and Spain mutually relinquish all claims for indemnity, national and individual, of every kind, of either Government, or of its citizens or subjects, against the other Government, that

may have arisen since the beginning of the late insurrection in Cuba
and prior to the exchange of ratifications of the present treaty, including
all claims for indemnity for the cost of the war.

The United States will adjudicate and settle the claims of its citizens against Spain relinquished in this article.

Article VIII.

In conformity with the provisions of Articles I, II, and III of this
treaty, Spain relinquishes in Cuba, and cedes in Porto Rico and other
islands in the West Indies, in the island of Guam, and in the Philippine
Archipelago, all the buildings, wharves, barracks, forts, structures, public
highways and other immovable property which, in conformity with law,
belong to the public domain, and as such belong to the Crown of Spain.

And it is hereby declared that the relinquishment or cession, as
the case may be, to which the preceding paragraph refers, can not in
any respect impair the property or rights which by law belong to the
peaceful possession of property of all kinds, of provinces, municipalities, public or private establishments, ecclesiastical or civic bodies, or
any other associations having legal capacity to acquire and possess
property in the aforesaid territories renounced or ceded, or of private
individuals, of whatsoever nationality such individuals may be.

The aforesaid relinquishment or cession, as the case may be,
includes all documents exclusively referring to the sovereignty relinquished or ceded that may exist in the archives of the Peninsula. Where
any document in such archives only in part relates to said sovereignty, a
copy of such part will be furnished whenever it shall be requested. Like
rules shall be reciprocally observed in favor of Spain in respect of documents in the archives of the islands above referred to.

In the aforesaid relinquishment or cession, as the case may be, are
also included such rights as the Crown of Spain and its authorities possess in respect of the official archives and records, executive as well as
judicial, in the islands above referred to, which relate to said islands or
the rights and property of their inhabitants. Such archives and records
shall be carefully preserved, and private persons shall without distinction have the right to require, in accordance with law, authenticated
copies of the contracts, wills and other instruments forming part of
notorial protocols or files, or which may be contained in the executive
or judicial archives, be the latter in Spain or in the islands aforesaid.

Article IX.

Spanish subjects, natives of the Peninsula, residing in the territory over which Spain by the present treaty relinquishes or cedes her sovereignty, may remain in such territory or may remove therefrom, retaining in either event all their rights of property, including the right to sell or dispose of such property or of its proceeds; and they shall also have the right to carry on their industry, commerce and professions, being subject in respect thereof to such laws as are applicable to other foreigners. In case they remain in the territory they may preserve their allegiance to the Crown of Spain by making, before a court of record, within a year from the date of the exchange of ratifications of this treaty, a declaration of their decision to preserve such allegiance; in default of which declaration they shall be held to have renounced it and to have adopted the nationality of the territory in which they may reside.

The civil rights and political status of the native inhabitants of the territories hereby ceded to the United States shall be determined by the Congress.

Article X.

The inhabitants of the territories over which Spain relinquishes or cedes her sovereignty shall be secured in the free exercise of their religion.

Article XI.

The Spaniards residing in the territories over which Spain by this treaty cedes or relinquishes her sovereignty shall be subject in matters civil as well as criminal to the jurisdiction of the courts of the country wherein they reside, pursuant to the ordinary laws governing the same; and they shall have the right to appear before such courts, and to pursue the same course as citizens of the country to which the courts belong.

Article XII.

Judicial proceedings pending at the time of the exchange of ratifications of this treaty in the territories over which Spain relinquishes or cedes her sovereignty shall be determined according to the following rules:

1. Judgments rendered either in civil suits between private individuals, or in criminal matters, before the date mentioned, and with respect to which there is no recourse or right of review under the Spanish law, shall be deemed to be final, and shall be executed in due form by competent authority in the territory within which such judgments should be carried out.
2. Civil suits between private individuals which may on the date mentioned be undetermined shall be prosecuted to judgment before the court in which they may then be pending or in the court that may be substituted therefor.
3. Criminal actions pending on the date mentioned before the Supreme Court of Spain against citizens of the territory which by this treaty ceases to be Spanish shall continue under its jurisdiction until final judgment; but, such judgment having been rendered, the execution thereof shall be committed to the competent authority of the place in which the case arose.

Article XIII.

The rights of property secured by copyrights and patents acquired by Spaniards in the Island of Cuba and in Porto Rico, the Philippines and other ceded territories, at the time of the exchange of the ratifications of this treaty, shall continue to be respected. Spanish scientific, literary and artistic works, not subversive of public order in the territories in question, shall continue to be admitted free of duty into such territories, for the period of ten years, to be reckoned from the date of the exchange of the ratifications of this treaty.

Article XIV.

Spain will have the power to establish consular officers in the ports and places of the territories, the sovereignty over which has been either relinquished or ceded by the present treaty.

Article XV.

The Government of each country will, for the term of ten years, accord to the merchant vessels of the other country the same treatment in respect of all port charges, including entrance and clearance dues, light dues, and tonnage duties, as it accords to its own merchant vessels, not engaged in the coastwise trade.

Article XVI.

It is understood that any obligations assumed in this treaty by the United States with respect to Cuba are limited to the time of its occupancy thereof; but it will upon termination of such occupancy, advise any Government established in the island to assume the same obligations.

Article XVII.

The present treaty shall be ratified by the President of the United States, by and with the advice and consent of the Senate thereof, and by Her Majesty the Queen Regent of Spain; and the ratifications shall be exchanged at Washington within six months from the date hereof, or earlier if possible. In faith whereof, we, the respective Plenipotentiaries, have signed this treaty and have hereunto affixed our seals. Done in duplicate at Paris, the tenth day of December, in the year of Our Lord one thousand eight hundred and ninety-eight.

[Seal] William R. Day
[Seal] Cushman K. Davis
[Seal] William P. Frye
[Seal] George Gray [Seal] Whitelaw Reid
[Seal] Eugenio Montero Rios
[Seal] B. de Abarzuzal [Seal] J. de Garnica
[Seal] W. R. de Villa Urrutia
[Seal] Rafael Cerero

Source: *A Treaty of Peace Between the United States and Spain,* U.S. Congress, 55th Congress, Third Sess., Senate Doc. no. 62, part 1 (Washington, D.C.: U.S. Government Printing Office, 1899), pp. 5–11.

Document 14
McKinley's Proclamation of "Benevolent Assimilation" to the People of the Philippines, December 21, 1898

Believing that the people of the Philippines were incapable of self-government and claiming never to have offered to aid Emilio Aguinaldo in his quest for independence, the president attempted to reassure the Filipinos of his benevolent intentions. He failed because by this time the treaty had been signed and Aguinaldo was certain he had been betrayed. War was practically inevitable.

In performing this duty [the extension of American sovereignty throughout the Philippines by means of force] the military commander of the United States is enjoined to make known to the inhabitants of the Philippine Islands that in succeeding to the sovereignty of Spain, in severing the former political relations, and in establishing a new political power, the authority of the United States is to be exerted for the securing of the persons and property of the people of the Islands and for the confirmation of all private rights and relations. It will be the duty of the commander of the forces of occupation to announce and proclaim in the most public manner that we come not as invaders or conquerors, but as friends, to protect the natives in their homes, in their employment, and in their personal and religious rights. All persons who, either by active aid or by honest submission, cooperate with the Government of the United States to give effect to these beneficent purposes will receive the reward of its support and protection. All others will be brought within the lawful rule we have assumed, with firmness if need be, but without severity, so far as may be possible. . . .

Finally, it should be the earnest and paramount aim of the military administration to win the confidence, respect, and affection of the inhabitants of the Philippines by assuring them in every possible way that full measure of individual rights and liberties which is the heritage of a free people, and by proving to them that the mission of the United States is one of the benevolent assimilation, substituting the mild sway of justice and right for arbitrary rule. In the fulfillment of this high mission, supporting the temperate administration of affairs for the greatest good of the governed, there must be sedulously maintained the strong arm of authority, to repress disturbance and to overcome all obstacles to the bestowal of the blessings of good and stable government upon the people of the Philippine Islands under the flag of the United States.

Source: 19. Benevolent Assimilation Proclamation—U.S. Army Center for Military History, Correspondence Relating to the War With Spain Including the Insurrection in the Philippine Islands and the China Relief Expedition: April 15, 1898, to July 30, 1902 (Washington, D.C.: U.S. Government Printing Office, 1993), pp. 858–59.

Document 15
The Platt Amendment

Although the United States went to war in 1898 to save the Cubans from Spanish oppression, the government was reluctant simply to evacuate Cuba when hostilities ended. That action might have led to unwanted complications such as possible intervention by another power. The policy that was followed was formulated by Secretary of War Elihu Root and embodied in a document known as the Platt Amendment, a rider on the army appropriation bill of March 2, 1901. It bore the name of Senator Orville Platt of Connecticut, who sponsored it in the upper house. Root had attempted a bit earlier to persuade the Cubans to include the provisions of the amendment in the new constitution, but they refused. However, when they were informed that acceptance was mandatory before U.S. military forces would withdraw, they accepted. Cuba thus became for all practical purposes a protectorate of the United States. The terms of the amendment were incorporated into a treaty between the United States and Cuba in 1903 and into the Cuban constitution of the same year. General Leonard Wood, U.S. military commander in Cuba at the time, believed the terms of the Platt Amendment would soon lead to outright annexation and so did most Cubans, but this did not happen. Nevertheless, the Platt Amendment governed U.S.-Cuban relations until 1934. What follows are the important articles of the amendment.

THE PLATT AMENDMENT, 1903

Article I. The Government of Cuba shall never enter into any treaty or other compact with any foreign power or powers which will impair or tend to impair the independence of Cuba, nor in any manner authorize or permit any foreign power or powers to obtain by colonization or for military or naval purposes, or otherwise, lodgment in or control over any portion of said island.

Article II. The Government of Cuba shall not assume or contract any public debt to pay the interest upon which, and to make reasonable sinking-fund provision for the ultimate discharge of which, the ordinary revenues of the Island of Cuba, after defraying the current expenses of the Government, shall be inadequate.

Article III. The Government of Cuba consents that the United States may exercise the right to intervene for the preservation of Cuban independence, the maintenance of a government adequate for the protection of life, property, and individual liberty, and for discharging the obligations with respect to Cuba imposed by the Treaty of Paris on the United States, now to be assumed and undertaken by the Government of Cuba. . . .

Article V. The Government of Cuba will execute, and, as far as necessary, extend the plans already devised, or other plans to be mutually agreed upon, for the sanitation of the cities of the island, to the end that a recurrence of epidemic and infectious diseases may be prevented, thereby assuring protection to the people and commerce of Cuba, as well as to the commerce of the Southern ports of the United States and the people residing therein. . . .

Article VII. To enable the United States to maintain the independence of Cuba, and to protect the people thereof, as well as for its own defense, the Government of Cuba will sell or lease to the United States lands necessary for coaling or naval stations, at certain specified points, to be agreed upon with the President of the United States.

Source: C. I. Blevans, ed., 19. Platt Amendment—"The Platt Amendment," in *Treaties and Other International Agreements of the United States of America, 1776–1949,* vol. 8 (Washington, D.C.: U.S. Government Printing Office, 1971), pp. 1116–17.

ANNOTATED BIBLIOGRAPHY

Books

Azoy, A. C. M. *Signal 250! The Sea Fight Off Santiago.* New York: David McKay, 1964. Account of the American naval victory near Santiago, Cuba in 1898.

Bemis, Samuel Flagg. *A Diplomatic History of the United States,* 5th ed. New York: Holt, Rinehart and Winston, 1965. Bemis was long the dear of American diplomatic historians. This book is one of the finest surveys of that subject.

Benton, Elbert J. *International Law and Diplomacy of the Spanish-American War.* Baltimore: Johns Hopkins Press, 1908. History of the relations of the United States and Spain during the Cuban insurrection and the resulting war. Emphasis is given to the debatable points of international law that arose during the conflict. The author contends that the *reconcentrados* policy was justifiable, that the *Maine* case should have been submitted to arbitration, and that McKinley did not exhaust the resources of diplomacy before resorting to force.

Berbusse, Edward J. *The United States in Puerto Rico, 1898–1900.* Chapel Hill: University of North Carolina Press, 1966. Emphasizes the tensions and essential changes that occurred during the last years of Spain's hegemony and the first years of U.S. sovereignty in Puerto Rico.

Brands, H. W. *The Reckless Decade: America in the 1890s.* New York: St. Martin's Press, 1995. Survey of the 1890s, concentrating on economic and political topics. Most of the book deals with domestic affairs in the United States. However, the last chapter covers the American transformation from a regional power early in the decade to an emerging global power at the end of the Spanish-American War.

Buenzle, Fred J. *Bluejacket: An Autobiography.* Annapolis, Md.: Naval Institute Press, 1986. Reprint of the original 1939 edition. Covers the years from the author's enlistment in 1899, at age 16, until the battle of Santiago.

Carr, Raymond. *Modern Spain, 1875–1980.* Oxford: Oxford University Press, 1980. First work in the English language to cover the history of contemporary Spain, from the restoration of the constitutional monarchy in 1875 to its second restoration and its present king, Juan Carlos.

Chadwick, French E. *The Relations of the United States and Spain: The Spanish-American War.* New York: Charles Scribner's Sons, 1911. Documentary history of the Spanish-American War with emphasis on naval activities. Chadwick was a naval officer who participated in most of the events he describes.

Clark, Charles E. *My Fifty Years in the Navy.* Annapolis, Md.: Naval Institute Press, 1984. Reprint of original 1917 edition. Story of the author's life from graduation from the naval academy in 1863 until his retirement from active duty in 1905.

Clymer, Kenton J. *John Hay: The Gentleman as Diplomat.* Ann Arbor: University of Michigan Press, 1975. Study of a man who began his public life as private secretary to Lincoln and ended his career as secretary of state under T. R. Roosevelt. The work is very sympathetic to Hay.

Coolidge, Louis A. *Orville H. Platt: An Old Fashioned Senator of Connecticut.* New York: G. P. Putnam's Sons, 1910. Details the public life of the author of the Platt Amendment. The author believes Platt closely approached being the perfect public servant—he was above temptation to profit materially from his office and performed his duties without thought to any personal or political effect on him.

Cortissoz, Royal. *The Life of Whitelaw Reid.* Two volumes. New York: Charles Scribner's Sons, 1921. Based on Reid's correspondence, covers his work as editor and proprietor of the *New York Tribune,* ambassador to France, and ambassador to Great Britain.

Dawes, Charles G. *A Journal of the McKinley Years.* Edited by Bascom N. Timmons. Chicago: Lakeside Press, 1950. Discusses politics, business, and social life in Washington, D.C.; Chicago; and New York from 1892 to 1913.

De Conde, Alexander. *A History of American Foreign Policy.* New York: Charles Scribner's Sons, 1963. DeConde was another of the great diplomatic historians. This book is an excellent survey.

Dennett, Tyler. *John Hay: From Poetry to Politics.* New York: Dodd, Mead, 1934. Wonderful biography of Hay that captures all the facets of his life including his education, his public service, his business career, and his literary career. Concludes that Hay was a remarkable man of many talents, successful in all, who cannot be placed in any particular niche.

Dewey, George. *Autobiography of George Dewey.* Annapolis, Md.: Naval Institute Press, 1987; originally published in 1913 by Charles Scribner's Sons, New York. Account of Admiral Dewey's naval career from his days as a midshipman at the U.S. Naval Academy through the taking of Manila during the Spanish-American War. There is little dealing with his life before the naval academy or after the war. Dewey says he wrote it for the sake of historical accuracy, but much of it is self-serving.

Dyal, Donald H., Brian B. Carpenter, and Mark Thomas. *Historical Dictionary of the Spanish American War.* Westport, Conn.: Greenwood, 1996. Resource volume useful in identifying the role of people, organizations, and places in the Spanish-American War.

Ellis, Elmer. *Henry Moore Teller, Defender of the West.* Caldwell, Idaho: Caxton Printers, 1941. Biography of the Senator from Colorado. Looks at the role of the American West in national affairs. The author believes Teller looked beyond local interests and was a strong nationalist.

Foner, Philip S. *The Spanish-Cuban-American War and the Birth of American Imperialism, 1895–1902.* Two volumes. New York: Monthly Review Press, 1972. Deals with the Spanish-Cuban-American War, the occupation of Cuba, and the imposition of the Platt Amendment. The book examines the overthrow of Spanish rule in Cuba and how the Cubans' victory was not realized because of American imperialism.

Freidel, Frank. *The Splendid Little War.* Boston: Little, Brown and Company, 1958. History of the Spanish-American War through the writings, drawings, and pictures of the correspondents who covered it. Contains many photographs and quotes by the participants.

Garraty, John A. *Henry Cabot Lodge: A Biography.* New York: Alfred A. Knopf, 1953. Biography of Henry Cabot Lodge that involved the first-time use of the family's private papers. The author attempts to strike a middle ground in his appraisal by both praising and criticizing Lodge's work and actions.

Gilderhus, Mark T. *The Second Century: U.S.-Latin American Relations Since 1889.* Wilmington, Del.: Scholarly Resources, 2000. Discusses U.S.–Latin American relations since 1889 in terms of both U.S. policy and Latin American reaction. The conclusions are balanced and fair to both sides.

Goldberg, Joyce S., *The Baltimore Affair.* Lincoln: University of Nebraska, 1986. Account of a confrontation between Chilean civilians and American sailors from the USS *Baltimore* on shore leave in Valparaíso, Chile, in 1891. It includes a discussion of the deaths of two sailors, and of the political consequences of the incident. Winifred Scott Schley was in command. He was commended for his handling of the dangerous affair.

Gould, Lewis L. *The Presidency of William McKinley.* Lawrence: Regents Press of Kansas, 1980. Discussion of the coming of the Spanish-American War,

McKinley's conduct of it, and the emergence of the American empire from 1898 to 1900.

Harbaugh, William H. *Power and Responsibility: The Life and Times of Theodore Roosevelt.* New York: Farrar, Straus, and Cudahy, 1961. Although old, Harbaugh's work is not outdated. It is still regarded as one of the best biographies of Theodore Roosevelt.

Healy, David. *Drive to Hegemony: The United States in the Caribbean, 1898–1917.* Madison: University of Wisconsin Press, 1988. Account of the United States' rise to dominate the Caribbean from 1898 to 1917. It does not cover Mexico; Columbia; Venezuela; or the Caribbean colonies of Great Britain, France, and the Netherlands. Looks at the techniques developed to exercise hegemony over the small sovereign states of the area, the reasons the United States wanted hegemony, and the effects from its establishment.

Healy, Laurin Hall, and Luis Kutner. *The Admiral.* New York: Ziff Davis, 1944. Interweaves Admiral George Dewey's naval career with a history of the U.S. navy. This was the first work to have access to the Sargent Report, which dealt with Dewey's activities during the Spanish-American War.

Hendrickson, Kenneth E. Jr. "Reluctant Expansionist—Jacob Gould Shurman and the Philippine Question." *Pacific Historical Review* 36 (1967): pp. 405–21. This article is the only detailed account of the Shurman mission.

Hilderbrand, Robert. *Power and the People: Executive Management of Public Opinion, 1897–1921.* Chapel Hill: University of North Carolina Press, 1981. Traces the use of presidential power to direct popular attitudes under McKinley, Theodore Roosevelt, Taft, and Wilson.

Hoyt, Edwin P. *The Lonely Ships: The Life and Death of the U.S. Asiatic Squadron.* New York: David McKay, 1976. History of the U.S. Asiatic Squadron from the 1850s until its demise in 1942.

Jessup, Phillip C. *Elihu Root.* Two volumes. New York: Dodd, Mead, 1938. Biography of the secretary of war and later secretary of state in the Roosevelt administration. The author had full access to Root's papers and conducted oral interviews on some of the topics. Though Root approved of the author doing the work, he made no attempt to influence it. The book is generally objective.

Jones, Stanley L. *The Presidential Election of 1896.* Madison: University of Wisconsin Press, 1964. Well-balanced and nonpartisan account of one of the most important elections in American history.

Jones, Virgil Carrington. *Roosevelt's Rough Riders.* Garden City, N.Y.: Doubleday, 1971. Account of Roosevelt's Rough Riders from the standpoint of a man in the ranks. It is an enthusiastic and often sentimental account of the unit. Jones overlooks much of the incompetence of the Spanish and the good luck of the Americans in Cuba.

Kelley, Alfred H., and Winfred A. Harbison. *The American Constitution: Its Origins and Development.* 3d ed. New York: Norton, 1963. A classic, this book has always been regarded as the leading summary of U.S. Constitutional history and law.

Kohlsaat, Herman H. *From McKinley to Harding: Personal Recollections of Our Presidents.* New York: Charles Scribner's Sons, 1923. Reprints of a series of reminiscences first published in the *Saturday Evening Post* covering the presidents, conventions, and other political events of the period.

Kushner, Howard I., and Anne Hummel Sherrill. *John Milton Hay: The Union of Poetry and Politics.* New York: Twayne, 1977. Essay on the life of John Hay, explaining how the son of a rural physician rose to direct the foreign policy of the United States.

LaFeber, Walter. *The New Empire: An Interpretation of American Expansionism, 1860–1898.* Ithaca: Cornell University Press, 1963. A look at American foreign policy from 1860 to 1898, arguing that it was driven by a desire for new or expanded overseas markets.

Leech, Margaret. *In the Days of McKinley.* New York: Harper and Brothers, 1959. Combines a biography of McKinley with a portrait of his era. It is sympathetic to McKinley.

LeJeune, John A. *The Reminiscences of a Marine.* Philadelphia: Dorrance, 1930. Autobiographical story of the 41-year Marine Corps career of General John A. Lejeune, 13th Commander of the Marine Corps and Commanding General of the Second Army Division in World War I.

Lewis, Cleona. *America's Stake in International Investments.* Washington, D.C.: Brookings Institute, 1938. Study of international financial relations emphasizing the United States' evolution from a weak debtor nation to a wealthy world power.

Linderman, Gerald F. *The Mirror of War: American Society and the Spanish-American War.* Ann Arbor: University of Michigan Press, 1974. A look at American society at the time of the Spanish-American War. Explains that a general consensus of public opinion existed concerning U.S. foreign policy until it became clear that overseas possessions were to be seized. After that some opposition emerged, but it was drowned out by the enthusiasm for expansion.

Linn, Brian McAllister, *The Philippine War, 1899–1902.* Modern War Studies series. Lawrence: University Press of Kansas, 2000. History of military operations in the Philippines. The first half of the book deals with conventional operations during 1899 and the second half with guerrilla warfare and pacification campaigns. Focuses on American operations, using U.S. records; however, some Philippine secondary literature and captured guerrilla records are used.

Lodge, Henry C., ed. *Selections from the Correspondence of Theodore Roosevelt and Henry Cabot Lodge, 1884–1918.* Two volumes. New York: Charles

Scribner's Son, 1925. Key correspondence between the two men from 1884 to 1918.The selections from the Spanish-American War are very revealing for they show clearly that Roosevelt and Lodge were expansionists.

Long, John Davis. *America of Yesterday, As Reflected in the Journal of John Davis Long.* Edited by Lawrence Shaw Mayo. Boston: Atlantic Monthly Press, 1923. The life of Secretary of the Navy John D. Long as reflected in his diary. The section on the Spanish-American War reveals that Long was a skilled administrator.

May, Ernest R. *Imperial Democracy: The Emergence of America as a Great Power.* New York: Harcourt, Brace and World, 1961. Account of American imperialism and the Spanish-American War. Emphasizes the development of expansionist policy.

McCullough, David. *Mornings on Horseback.* New York: Simon and Schuster, 1981. A look at Roosevelt's family and life until "he was formed as a person," as a result of his defeat in the New York mayoral election of 1886. The author is a wonderful writer and the account is very engaging.

McElroy, Robert. *Grover Cleveland: The Man and the Statesman.* New York: Harper and Brothers, 1923. This old but still useful volume contains a detailed account of Cleveland's policies.

Millis, Walter. *The Martial Spirit: A Study of Our War With Spain.* Cambridge: Riverside Press, 1931. Study of the Spanish-American War, from the second insurrection in Cuba in 1895 until the ratification of the Peace of Paris in 1899. Covers the roles of influential leaders and their parts in prodding the nation into the belligerency. It is a lighthearted account and contains very superficial analysis.

Milton, Joyce. *The Yellow Kids: Foreign Correspondents in the Heyday of Yellow Journalism.* New York: Harper and Row, 1989. Reexamination of the role of the "yellow kid" correspondents in Cuba. Discusses whether everything that was said about them or supposedly done by them was true.

Miner, D. C. *The Fight for the Panama Route: The Story of the Spooner Act and the Hay-Herrán Treaty.* New York: Octagon Books, 1971. This book is the definitive study of the process by means of which the canal route through Panama was chosen.

Morales Carrión, Arturo. *Puerto Rico: A Political and Cultural History.* New York: Norton and Company, 1983. History of Puerto Rico from Indian and Spanish colonial times to the commonwealth. The island has been termed a commonwealth since 1952, but the term is essentially meaningless.

Morgan, H. Wayne. *William McKinley and His America.* Syracuse, N.Y.: Syracuse University Press, 1963. Critical biography that differs from the popular image of the 25th president of the United States.

Musicant, Ivan. *Empire by Default: The Spanish-American War and the Dawn of the American Century.* New York: Henry Holt and Company, 1998. Presents a military history of the Spanish-American War, arguing that the acquisition of empire was an unplanned result.

Offner, John L. *An Unwanted War: The Diplomacy of the United States and Spain Over Cuba, 1895–1898.* Chapel Hill: University of North Carolina Press, 1992. A look at the American, Spanish, and Cuban diplomatic perspectives of the Spanish-American struggle over Cuba. The book shows clearly how a war that nobody wanted became inevitable.

Olcott, Charles S. *The Life of William McKinley.* Two volumes. Boston: Houghton Mifflin, 1916. Biography based on information gleaned from friends and associates; McKinley did not keep a diary and was a disappointing letter writer. Contains little useful analysis.

O'Toole, George J. A. *The Spanish War, An American Epic—1898.* New York: W. W. Norton, 1984. Covers the causes and execution of the war as well as the peace treaty of 1898. Contains many quotes but is quite superficial.

Payne, Stanley G. *Politics and the Military in Modern Spain.* Stanford, Calif.: Stanford University Press, 1967. Study of the relation of the military to Spanish politics, government, and public issues in the nineteenth and twentieth centuries.

———. *A History of Spain and Portugal.* Two volumes. Madison: University of Wisconsin Press, 1973. Volume Two takes the Iberian peninsula from the Bourbon regime of the eighteenth century to the date of publication and covers its political, social, economic, and cultural history.

Pérez, Louis A. Jr. *Cuba and the United States: Ties of Singular Intimacy.* Athens: University of Georgia Press, 1990. Discusses the commercial relationship between Cuba and the United States during the eighteenth century and goes on to cover slavery, Manifest Destiny, attempts to purchase the island, and the Spanish-American War and its results.

Perusse, Roland J. *The United States and Puerto Rico: The Struggle for Equality.* Malabar, Fla.: Robert E. Krieger, 1990. This excellent book traces the quest for political equality and civil liberty in Puerto Rico from the time of American conquest to the late twentieth century.

Poyo, Gerald E. *"With All, and for the Good of All": The Emergence of Popular Nationalism in the Cuban Communities of the United States, 1848–1898.* Durham, N.C.: Duke University Press, 1989. Examination of the role of U.S. Cuban communities in the growth and consolidation of nineteenth-century Cuban nationalism.

Pratt, Julius W. *Expansionists of 1898: The Acquisition of Hawaii and the Spanish Islands.* Baltimore: Johns Hopkins Press, 1936. Reprint. Baltimore: Peter Smith, 1949. Series of lectures, delivered at the Walter Hines Page School of International Relations of Johns Hopkins University, covering the most important period of imperialism for the United States—from the Harrison administration until the annexation of Hawaii.

Reuter, Bertha Ann. *Anglo-American Relations During the Spanish-American War.* New York: MacMillan, 1924. Study of the diplomatic relations between the United States and Great Britain based on an examination of official documents and contemporary public opinion expressed in the periodical literature of the day.

Reynolds, Francis J. *The United States Navy.* New York: P. F. Collier & Son, 1918. A pictorial history of the United States Navy from 1775 until 1918.

Rhodes, James F. *The McKinley and Roosevelt Administrations, 1897–1909.* New York: Macmillan, 1922. Begins with the campaign and election of 1896 and cover the period until the campaign and election of 1900. The middle chapters covers the background of the Spanish-American War, the war itself, and its aftermath.

Robinson, William A. *Thomas B. Reed: Parliamentarian.* New York: Dodd, Mead, 1930. Biography of Thomas B. Reed, lawyer, member of the House of Representatives from 1877 to 1899, and Speaker of the House for three congresses. The author endeavors to let Reed tell his own story, explain his own course, and give his opinions on the issues of his day. Also shown here is how Reed appeared to his contemporaries. The author presents the facts and lets readers draw their own conclusions.

Roosevelt, Theodore. *The Letters of Theodore Roosevelt: The Years of Preparations, 1868–1900.* Edited by Elting E. Morison et al. Two volumes. Cambridge: Harvard University Press, 1951. Letters by Theodore Roosevelt from 1868, when he was 10, until 1900. The first two volumes of an eight-volume set.

———. *An Autobiography.* New York: Macmillan, 1919. Roosevelt's life through the date of publication. It is, of course, very self-serving.

———. *The Rough Riders.* New York: Charles Scribner's Sons, 1902. Reprint, Da Capo Paperback, 1990. The story of the First United States Volunteer Cavalry as told by its leader and most famous member.

Rubens, Horatio S. *Liberty: The Story of Cuba.* New York: Brewer, Warren and Putnam, 1932. Rubens, a friend and advisor to Cuban patriot José Martí and counsel general for the Cuban revolutionary council in America, wrote this account of Cuba's struggle for freedom. It is, of course, very sympathetic to the Cuban cause for independence.

Samuels, Peggy and Harold Samuels. *Remembering the* Maine. Washington, D.C.: Smithsonian Institution Press, 1995. Account of the career of the battleship *Maine* from the day it was launched in November 1885 until the day it went down in February 1898.

———. *Teddy Roosevelt at San Juan: The Making of a President.* College Station: Texas A&M University Press, 1997. Survey of the era and a specific event focusing on Theodore Roosevelt and the Battle of San Juan Hill. Narrative shifts back and forth in time, as it addresses the development of the First United States Volunteer Cavalry and Roosevelt's personal development.

Schroeder, Seaton. *A Half Century of Naval Service.* New York: D. Appleton, 1922. Covers the author's naval service from Annapolis (class of 1868) through his retirement in 1911. He took part in all the important Atlantic Fleet activities during the period.

Schubert, Frank N. *Black Valor, Buffalo Soldiers and the Medal of Honor, 1870–1898.* Wilmington, Del.: Scholarly Resources, 1997. The author, a Department of Defense historian, offers accounts of African Americans who won the Congressional Medal of Honor during the Indian wars and the Spanish-American War.

Sigsbee, Charles D. *The Maine, an Account of her Destruction in Havana Harbor: Personal Narrative.* New York: Century, 1899. The sinking of the ship as told by her commanding officer. Sigsbee was convinced that the cause of the disaster was sabotage.

Spector, Ronald. *Admiral of the New Empire: The Life and Career of George Dewey.* Baton Rouge: Louisiana State University Press, 1974. Scholarly look at Dewey's life and career using Navy Department records and family correspondence. Believes Dewey's career may have been more representative of the Naval Officer Corps of his time than that of Mahan or Sims. Also, through Dewey's naval career, the author looks at American naval policy from 1900 until the time of Dewey's retirement.

Suchliki, Jaime. *Cuba from Columbus to Castro.* New York: Charles Scribner's Sons, 1974. A survey of Cuban history from discovery to modern times.

Trask, David F. *The War with Spain in 1898.* New York: Macmillian, 1981. Detailed look at the conduct of the war with Spain and its political and geographical consequences. The definitive work on the subject.

Traxel, David. *1898: The Birth of the American Century.* New York: Knopf, 1998. According to the author, the year 1898 was pivotal in American history. Traxel discusses the events of that year, including the Spanish-American War, the growth of large corporations, advancements in technology, and labor strife as they contributed to the birth of modern America as a great power.

Tyler, Sydney. *The Japan-Russia War.* Harrisburg, Penn.: Minister, 1905. This early commentary describes the Russo-Japanese war as "the greatest conflict of modern times."

Walker, Dale L. *The Boys of '98 : Theodore Roosevelt and the Rough Riders.* New York: St. Martin's, 1998. Succinct biographical sketches of politicians, soldiers, and sailors, along with a well- organized analysis of the war's causes, the role of the newspapers and their staffs, and the tactics and strategies of the combatants. Includes interviews with the last three surviving Rough Riders.

Webber, Bert. *Battleship Oregon: Bulldog of the Navy.* Medford, Mass.: Webb Research Group, 1994. Discusses the battleship *Oregon's* activities during the Spanish-American War, especially the epic voyage around Cape Horn.

West, Richard S. Jr. *Admirals of American Empire.* New York: Bobbs-Merrill, 1948. Combined biographies of admirals George Dewey, Albert Thayer Mahan, Winfield Scott Scheley, and William Thomas Sampson, all midshipmen at the naval academy at the same time, through the decline, rebirth, and final emergence of the new navy.

Wilkerson, Marcus W. *Public Opinion and the Spanish-American War.* Baton Rouge: Louisiana State University Press, 1932. Study of war propaganda in the *New York World* and the *New York Journal* in the three years prior to the Spanish-American War.

Williams, T. Harry. *The History of American Wars.* New York: Knopf, 1981. Williams' book contains a summary of all American wars. The essay on the Spanish-American War is one of the best.

Wisan, Joseph. *The Cuban Crisis as Reflected in the New York Press (1895–1898).* New York: Columbia University Press, 1934. Survey of the policies and activities of the New York press from February 1895 until April 1898. Essentially an analysis of yellow journalism, a major characteristic of the newspapers of the period.

Wooster, Robert. *Nelson A. Miles and the Twilight of the Frontier Army.* Lincoln: University of Nebraska Press, 1993. Covers Miles's career, emphasizing his roles in fighting Native Americans, in which he was very effective; and the Spanish-American War, in which his ideas and actions were very inconsistent.

Wriston, Henry M. *Executive Agents in American Foreign Relations.* Baltimore: Johns Hopkins Press, 1929. Delivered as the Albert Shaw Lectures on Diplomatic History in 1923; examines the use of diplomatic agents, by the president of the United States, to conduct specific items of foreign business without obtaining the consent of the Senate on their appointment. Stuart Woodford was an example.

Document Collections

Cervera y Topete, Pascual. *The Spanish-American War: A Collection of Documents Relative to the Squadron Operations in the West Indies.* Arranged by

Rear Admiral Pascual Cervera y Topete. Translated by the Office of Naval Intelligence. Washington, D.C.: Government Printing Office, 1900.

McKinley, William. *McKinley, The People's Choice: Full Text of Each Speech or Address Made by Him from June 18 to August 1, 1896.* Compiled by Joseph P. Smith. Canton, Ohio: Repository Press, 1896.

————. *McKinley's Speeches in August.* Compiled by Joseph P. Smith. Canton, Ohio: Repository Press, 1896.

————. *McKinley's Speeches in September.* Compiled by Joseph P. Smith. Canton, Ohio: Repository Press, 1896.

————. *McKinley's Speeches in October.* Compiled by Joseph P. Smith. Canton, Ohio: Repository Press, 1896.

[Spain, Minister of State.] *Spanish Diplomatic Correspondence and Documents, 1896–1900: Presented to the Cortes by the Minister of State.* [Translated by the United States.] Washington, D.C.: Government Printing Office, 1905.

U.S. Congress. *Congressional Record.* 54th Cong.,1st sess., 1895–96, 2d sess., 1896–97; 5th Cong., 1st sess., 1897, 2d sess., 1897–98.

————. Senate Committee on Foreign Relations. *Report Relative to Affairs in Cuba.* 55th Cong., 2d sess., S. Rept. 885. Serial 3624. Washington, D.C.: Government Printing Office, 1898.

U.S. Department of State. *Papers Relating to the Foreign Relations of the United States.* Washington, D.C.: Government Printing Office, 1897–1901.

U.S. Department of War. *Report of the Census of Cuba, 1899.* Washington, D.C.: Government Printing Office, 1900.

U.S. President. *Message in Response to the Resolution of the Senate, Dated February 14, 1898, Calling for Information in Respect to the Condition of "Reconcentrados" in Cuba, the State of War and the Country, and the Prospects of Projected Autonomy in that Island.* 55th Cong., 2d sess. S. Document 230. Serial 3610. Washington, D.C.: Government Printing Office, 1898.

U.S. Secretary of the Navy. *Annual Report of the Navy Department of the Year, 1898.* Washington, D.C.: Government Printing Office, 1898.

U.S. Secretary of State. *Report in Response to Senate Resolution, February 23, 1897, Relative to the Arrest, Imprisonment, and Death of Dr. Ricardo Ruiz in the Jail of Guanabacoa, on the Island of Cuba.* 54th Cong., 2d sess., March 4, 1897. S. Document 179. Serial 3471. Washington, D.C.: Government Printing Office, 1897.

Newspapers and Magazines

Literary Digest [New York], January 1, 1896–August 15, 1898.

Nation [New York], January 1, 1897–August 15, 1898.

New York Herald, January 1, 1897–August 15, 1898.

New York Times, January 1, 1897–August 15, 1898.

New York Tribune, January 1, 1897–August 15, 1898.

Washington Post, January 1, 1895–August 15, 1898.

Washington Star, January 1, 1895–August 15, 1898.

INDEX

About the Author

KENNETH E. HENDRICKSON JR. is Hardin Distinguished Professor of History at Midwestern State University. His books include *Hard Times in Oklahoma*, and *The Chief Executives of Texas*, among others.